This Too Is MuSiC

DATE DUE

DE 18 '03			
DE 08			

This Too Is MuSic

Rena Upitis

Queen's University
Kingston, Ontario

With a Foreword by
Seymour Papert

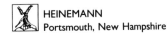
HEINEMANN
Portsmouth, New Hampshire

HEINEMANN EDUCATIONAL BOOKS, INC.
361 Hanover Street   Portsmouth, NH 03801
Offices and agents throughout the world

The author and publisher wish to thank the following for permission to reprint previously published material appearing in this book:

From James Herndon, *How to Survive in Your Native Land* (New York: Simon and Schuster, 1971), pp. 75, 29–31, 44–45. Copyright © 1971 by James Herndon. Reprinted by permission of the publisher.

From Jean Cochrane, *The One-Room School in Canada* (Toronto: Fitzberry & Whiteside Ltd., 1981), pp. 84–85. Reprinted by permission of Simon & Schuster.

Text from "Hector the Collector" from *Where the Sidewalk Ends* by Shel Silverstein. Copyright © 1974 by Evil Eye Music, Inc. Reprinted by permission of Harper & Row, Publishers, Inc.

Every effort has been made to contact the copyright holders and the children and their parents for permission to reprint borrowed material. We regret any oversights that may have occurred and would be happy to rectify them in future printings of this work.

Library of Congress Cataloging-in-Publication Data

Upitis, Rena Brigit.
    This too is music / Rena Upitis ; with a foreword by Seymour Papert.
        p.   cm.
    Includes bibliographical references (p.   ).
    ISBN 0-435-08539-5
    1. School music—Instruction and study.   I. Title.
MT1.U63   1990
372.87'044—dc20
                                                        90-4791
                                                            CIP
                                                            MN

Designed by Jenny Greenleaf.
Printed in the United States of America.
90 91 92 93 94 9 8 7 6 5 4 3 2 1

For Angus

*There are moments of connection
that we never forget*

Contents

Foreword

Seymour Papert

.... Many people will use this book as a source of ideas to help them teach music. Others will use it for ideas to help them teach—period. But those who will gain most from it will use it to think about themselves, about their own learning, and about learning itself. I know because Rena Upitis' work has served me in this way. Five years ago I was inspired (I can only call it that) to invite her to spend a year as a member of my research team in the MIT Media Laboratory. Images of learning gleaned from watching her work with children have become a permanent part of my thinking. Whenever I think about learning— or do some—I am aware of using her images.

Understanding learning is my lifelong passion. I have pursued it in many ways. I have read solemn theoretical treatises. I have even made theories of my own. But interestingly I find that what helps most is not the proliferation of abstract principles. I gain more by extending my collection of excellent "learnings"— concrete learning situations that I can use as "objects to think with."

And of such gems there is no richer source than Rena's work.

Just last week I was stuck trying to get the hang of a mathematical proof. After an hour of mental cramp, I closed my eyes, relaxed, and thought about Rena empowering children to improvise, drawing on musical knowledge they didn't know they had. I did the same for myself—and got it.

Is this "Socratic learning" or "Vygotskian learning" or what? Yes, it has something in common with the learnings these thinkers have taught us to recognize and label so we can talk to one another. But I'd just rather call it "Upitis learning."

Seymour Papert is Professor of Media Technology at Massachusetts Institute of Technology and the author of *Mindstorms: Children, Computers, and Powerful Ideas.*

Acknowledgments

·································· I have had much encouragement from my colleagues at MIT, at Queen's University, at the James W. Hennigan Community School, and from people in the Kingston music community. In particular, I thank Iain Craig, Mark Danby, Julia du Prey, Bill Egnatoff, Aaron Falbel, Bill Higginson, Linda Moriarty, Seymour Papert, June Simonson, and Alan Shaw. These people are much more than colleagues—they have been friends for some years now and have provided, unconditionally and unfailingly, personal and professional support when I needed it most.

The manuscript for this book was greatly enriched by criticism and advice from Glenda Bissex. I cannot thank her enough for the care that she took in reading several drafts and in suggesting modifications that undoubtedly added to the clarity of presentation.

The publication of this book was aided by many skilled and dedicated people associated with Heinemann Educational Books, Incorporated. I am especially indebted to Toby Gordon for her reliability, sensitivity, and wit. Thanks also to Donna Bouvier, whose job it was to oversee the final stages of production.

Finally, my thanks to the children who have taught me so much. I cannot begin to name the countless children who have been instrumental in shaping my thinking about teaching and learning. However, two should be named—both former students at the Hennigan—Frances Batuyios and my son, Damal Ray. Frannie and Damal not only challenged and expanded my notions of children's thinking, but encouraged me to write this book, prodding me frequently for progress reports when others were too polite to ask. Both Frannie and Damal read drafts in various stages, providing honest commentaries that were often much needed and certainly appreciated. In the final stages, Frannie exerted a good deal of energy in tracing the whereabouts of former students so that permission to use children's photographs and work could be obtained. The book would be far less lively without these contributions, and my thanks to Frannie for her help. A special thank you to Damal, and to the other members of my family, for the numerous sacrifices and "favors."

Just as no list of acknowledgments is ever complete, no work is ever finished—printed, perhaps, but not finished. As we were in the final stages of seeking permissions from parents, one child grabbed the composition she had created out from her mother's hand and dashed to the piano to read it from the standard notation. After she played it, she commented that she liked the way it began, but that she thought the ending could be improved. It is precisely in this spirit that this book is written. My thanks again, then, to all the children who have given much to me. Telling their stories is one way I hope to give something back.

This Too Is

On the Teaching of Music

"Music is a way of expressing your feelings."

"Hey! There's science in my math book. Have you ever thought about what it would be like if we had, like, one main teacher and one class all day, not separate, and we all had classes on, like, life?"

"Music is when you plan the sounds."

"All I know is, without music, people would be crazy."

Thoughts of fourth- to sixth-grade children

I HAVE never met anyone who disliked music. While we all have preferences for the styles of music we enjoy most, I suspect that very few of us have not been deeply moved by listening to music or making music in some way. I believe that it is also true that those who enjoy music the most have somehow learned to construct their own meaning from music, thereby in some way controlling their music-making activities, whether in improvisation, composition, performance, or simply listening to a piece of music. How, then, can we give teachers and children this kind of control and musical power? We have one strong factor in our favor in taking on the task of helping people become musicians, and that is, in some form *all of us are already musicians.*

I wrote this book because I am convinced that music can and should play a far more powerful role in the lives of children and their teachers in elementary schools. I am also convinced that teaching and learning about music need not lie in the hands of the "music specialists" alone, but should be a form of expression and learning that pervades the classroom environment, complementing and supplementing the work of the resident school music teacher. In order for this to happen, teachers need to realize that they have enough music background, from living with the music in our culture, to set conditions that make it possible for their students and for themselves to become better musicians.

I suspect that a good number of elementary school teachers would like to do more with music but feel that they lack the expertise to do so. Many, I am sure, have had some music experience—for example, taking piano lessons as children or strumming a few chords on a guitar—but haven't pursued those experiences. Unfortunately, because school music programs can be narrow in that they focus on singing and performance, it is sometimes difficult to see how one's limited out-of-school music experiences can relate to current classroom practice. As a teacher once told me, "Singing in the shower is one thing. Singing in the classroom is something else."

But while singing is important (see Chapter 10), there is more that can be done in the classroom with music than singing. In this book, I describe many ways for children and teachers to explore ideas and learn about music, often with a clear link to another subject domain. Therefore, the emphasis is not so much on "how to teach music", but rather on how music might be used as a subject to relate to all other disciplines. Thus, the hope is that teachers who read this book will find their own ways to relate music to the discipline that they like best, whether that discipline is science, math, language, visual art, or history. In working with classroom teachers to help them teach music in the ways that are described in this book, I have seen teachers with different strengths—language, science, or mathematics—reach the same ends with their children, but with different beginnings. For instance, much of the work with patterning that one sees in early primary mathematics can easily trigger work in music patterning, leading to improvised patterns, composition, and performance. Similarly, by beginning with poetry or chants or even single words, one can build musical shapes and forms. Ideas like these are described throughout the book.

It is important to note, however, that while the ways of approaching music described in these pages are potentially powerful ones, I have no intention of presenting a tried-and-true formula for success. This is not a fully detailed pedagogy on how to teach music or integrated arts. The process of learning how to do these things should itself be an evolving one, dependent on the teacher, the children, and the community of habits, beliefs, and ideas within which different ways of teaching music might be introduced.

For this reason, many of the anecdotes in this book illustrate my struggles with the inevitable difficulties in teaching, and in so doing, how my views of teaching and my views of myself as a musician have changed. For it is only in the last six or seven years that I have considered myself as a musician and composer, even though I have played the piano for over twenty years. I didn't think of myself as a musician because my performances were far from perfect—not at all the sense of "musician" that I use in this book. Similarly, while I composed music as a child, I soon stopped thinking of myself as a composer. Perhaps this was because I was made to realize as I grew older that I simply wasn't in the same class as Beethoven and Mozart. Unfortunately, we tend not to think of children as composers of music because we make judgments of their compositions based on adult standards. As Davies (1967) states:

> I have learned that, given favorable circumstances, the composition of music is no less natural for children than painting. We have become accustomed to children's painting, but their music is still suspect and we try to impose false standards upon children, which render its creation as unlikely as their pictorial art was a hundred years ago. (p. 33)

We are quick to praise young children's early writing, calling them writers at the outset, but it is simply not part of our practice to praise a seven-year-old's "plunking at the piano," calling him or her a musician. But surely part of the secret of becoming a musician or a composer (or whatever) is that one is encouraged to think that one already *is* those things. Not long ago, I started to learn to play the 'cello. Knowing I was a musician, someone asked me what instruments I played. I answered, "I'm a pianist and a 'cellist." Another colleague who was within earshot laughed and retorted, "Listen to her! She's had two lessons and already she's a 'cellist!" One becomes what one believes.

Before I embark on a description of ideas and environments that can be created in classrooms to bring music further into the lives of children, I would like to offer a description of the particular classroom where many of these ideas originated. I have since tried them in other classroom settings, working with other teachers and working with children on my own, and some modifications have been made. However, it is perhaps more important to describe in detail those early explorations I made along with the children, since it was during that time that most of the changes in my thinking and practice took place.

In the spring of 1985, I was invited to join the Learning and Epistemology Group at the Media Lab at the Massachusetts Institute of Technology in Cambridge, Massachusetts. My official title was something like Visiting Scholar or Research Associate, but, as most official titles go, the title tells little of what my time was really like in Cambridge. In fact, most of my waking hours were spent not in Cambridge at MIT, but in Roxbury at an inner-city elementary school.

The Hennigan School was selected as the site for a Technology School and "Project Headlight," a long-term research project of the Learning and Epistemology Group of the Media Lab at MIT. The Hennigan, an inner-city Boston school, had a diverse population, with Black, Hispanic, white, and Asian students. The majority of the students were Black and Hispanic. There was also a sizeable special needs population.

For the 250 children involved in the project, becoming a Technology School meant that several major changes took place in their school lives. First, over a hundred computers were brought into the school. These computers were used for creative writing, LOGO programming, Lego/LOGO, music, and in a number of other ways as tools to help build and create various products. The second major change brought about by Project Headlight was that these children found themselves in the company of some thirty graduate students and researchers, people like myself who took a genuine interest in the children's thoughts and feelings. The sheer number of extra people in the school as a result of Project Headlight meant that children had more opportunities than ever before to talk with people at school about what they were learning and thinking. I would venture to say that having so many interested people had at least as much effect on the children's intellectual and personal development as the presence of the computers. In fact, while the computer had a definite presence in the music classroom, the computer alone cannot explain the results described in this book. Rather, the computer was one of many tools that had a place in the Music Playground—Room 304 at the Hennigan School.

When I first walked into Room 304 I was overwhelmed by the sheer size of it. The room was almost bare—no desks, only a couple of chairs, one small shelf, and a movable blackboard. School was scheduled to start two days later. Other teachers were busy preparing their classrooms for the first day of school—arranging textbooks, pencils, paper, desks, tables, and chairs; creating multicolored and textured wall displays and bulletins; and removing unwanted debris from the previous year. My room had no chairs and tables because there was a shortage of furniture and other classrooms had priority. However, I was less concerned about the lack of furniture (I preferred to sit on the floor anyway) than I was about the lack of life in the classroom. There was no color—nothing enticing to touch or read or play—only a faded construction paper alphabet along the top of one of the blackboards. I strolled into the adjoining room to meet the teacher next door. She must have sensed my apprehension, for she offered to lend me materials and supplies to "brighten the place up a bit." I chatted with her for quite a while before going from her bright orange and yellow room back to my dark and drab blue and brown space. And then I began to cut and color, paint and paste.

As I was working, I contemplated what it would be like to have children in that room in less than forty-eight hours. I realized how unsure I was about teaching children in a school environment. I had years of formal music training, it was true, but very little classroom experience teaching music. While I had been teaching piano privately for over ten years, I knew it was going to be quite a different thing teaching music to a group of kids. Kids from a different country than mine. Kids from a different culture. To make matters worse, I had spent several years writing critical pieces about the inadequacies of public school music education, sitting safely at my desk in one prestigious university or another. I winced when I thought about how freely I had criticized, now that I found myself in the same position as "one of them." I had also spoken freely and often without much more than intuition and hope behind me, about how children would learn about music if they were composers themselves. I had even written a thesis on teaching music composition to children using computers, and conducted classroom research that "proved" that there was something to be said for using the computer as a composition tool. In fact, I wouldn't have been hired for this particular job had I not developed those ideas and shared them in the academic arena. But all of those things offered little in the way of reassurance or direction for facing some two hundred youngsters in a very new setting. How did one establish routines, discipline, and control when one was dealing with a group of new children? What techniques did one use to get kids interested? How would I look in the eyes of my MIT colleagues? Would I get fired from MIT?

Because I had been hired by a research group at MIT, my position at the Hennigan differed in many ways from those of other teachers. They recognized that I would not have been teaching at the school but for the project, and so they were ready to be somewhat flexible. I took advantage of their flexibility in order to survive the first few weeks (I was thinking of my job only in terms of survival at that point—stimulation and learning were the furthest things from my mind). I arranged, for the first three weeks, to see the children in small groups of six to eight in a group. Thus, the teachers sent a portion of their class at a time to Room 304, keeping the rest in their own classroom. I realized at the time that this meant considerable reorganization on the part of the teachers, and loss of some of their planning time. But it was a case of survival. I assured myself that I could handle any disaster with eight children much more easily than with twenty or more. Also, I figured that eight could never make as much noise as twenty, so at least it wouldn't sound as bad if anyone walked in unannounced. But most important of all, I knew that with only eight in the room I had a golden opportunity to get to know the children, even though the unusually small groups of eight were to last for only a short while. One of the greatest advantages in my private piano teaching was that I was able to establish strong personal ties with my students. This, to me, was the first and foremost goal of the initial meetings with the children.

As I sat at the piano playing a little bit of Bach the first morning of school, I realized that I still had no idea what I was going to do with the kids when they came through the door. I had only a meager smattering of approaches to "classroom music"—Orff, Kodaly, and some Dalcroze eurhythmics. Of the three, I knew most about Dalcroze. I had taken a Dalcroze course at the Manhattan School of Music just that summer, and so I had some notions of how movement might be used to enhance children's musical experiences and growth. I had heard about Orff and Kodaly in my university years, I knew what the pentatonic scale was, and I had improvised on the pentatonic scale as a child in school using Orff instruments. These things—a little bit of eurhythmics, the pentatonic scale, and Orff instruments—plus some familiarity with two computer composition programs (Musicland and Melody Manipulations; see Appendix) were all I felt that I had to draw upon that first day.

In retrospect, perhaps the most striking thing about my thinking during that early morning practice was the feeling that the music I was playing was somehow different from the music the kids would be making in school. At the time, my musical boundaries enclosed two kinds of music—private, "serious" performance and composition versus "school music." The two kinds of music, that first day, did not overlap. Now, only a few years later, the two circles overlap almost entirely. But at that time, despite all of my years of music training, I felt as inadequately equipped to teach music as someone with no training at all. In some ways, all of my classical training was a hindrance at first, and not a help. Perhaps I could play tunes readily on the piano, but a tape recorder could have been used to do this just as well. What good was all of that training in this environment? As it turned out, the first thing I decided to try was one of the Dalcroze exercises I had learned a few months before (see Chapter 3—Names Game). Fortunately, it worked so well that I concentrated on movement improvisations for quite some time, and by so doing, gradually all of the other pieces began to fall into place.

The more I began using different improvisation ideas, the more I thought about my own elementary school music experiences. I recalled and talked about one teacher in particular, from whom, in two short years, I had learned to sing many songs that I still enjoy today, from whom I had learned to play the soprano recorder, the guitar, how to write original ballads, and how to improvise on a variety of instruments. When someone asked me what her music background and experience was I admitted that I had no idea, but I assumed that it was extensive. My curiosity eventually prompted me to write to her, tracing her whereabouts through the elementary school I had attended some twenty years before. When she replied to my letter, I was at first surprised by her comments, but later realized that it made perfect sense that her own background was anything *but* extensive. She wrote:

When I first started teaching music over twenty years ago, I always suspected that someone would expose me as an imposter, but what a surprise that it would be a former Grade 5 student, now a professor at MIT!... When I began teaching music, it was because there was no one else in the school who was willing or able to do it. I had nothing more than a love for music and for song. We were fortunate, at the time, to have resources [e.g., Orff instruments] and a superb music consultant at the board, so I was well supported at the beginning. ... Since I did not read music, didn't play an instrument, it was not me but you who did the work, the learning. You were the ones who practiced, improvised, experimented, created. All I did was to set the conditions for you to make that possible.

I realize now that my music teacher was years ahead of her time. I remember well the improvisation and experimentation that she describes. I also remember that in her class we could work in small groups on instrumental ensembles, or sometimes choreographing a movement routine. While we still sat in desks arranged in rows during other classes, in music we worked much differently. We worked at centers, in "special spots" such as underneath the stage, and often on different activities of our own choice. Teachers now will recognize that such teaching practices reflected a child-centered activities approach to teaching and learning.

Perhaps one of the most prominent and positive changes we have witnessed in schools over the past two decades is the increasingly common view that education should be child-centered, that it should be relevant to the child's life and experiences. Along with this comes the view that subjects should be in some way integrated with each other, and with the larger aspects of people's lives. Thus, we see teachers dealing with topical issues such as acid rain, teaching their children how to solve problems rather than memorize strings of facts, and talking about and implementing a whole language approach, where language, written and oral, is not something separate from the stories of the children's lives. Some changes in the teaching of music have also begun to follow these lines, and this book is written in such a spirit. We need to continue to look for ways to make music, including improvisation and composition, accessible to children. One way of developing such musicianship is by integrating music, as modeled by the whole language approach, with all of the other subjects, particularly with the visual and dramatic arts. Earlier, I made the argument that linking music with other subjects could provide a way for classroom teachers to begin setting conditions for children to learn about music. But such an approach is also justified simply because music is not separate from other disciplines: it is a part of language, a part of mathematics, a part of movement, a part of dance. No subject, if studied deeply enough, is separate from the others.

I'm going to end this chapter with a question that I ask my incoming undergraduate students, who are taking their final pre-service teaching degree. I begin by saying, "Think of something you do well. This thing that you do well should be something that you pursue for enjoyment, something you have considerable knowledge about, something you might teach others to do, something that you continue to learn more and more about." Once everyone has something in mind I then ask, "How many have learned to do that thing in school?" Out of the thousands I have asked, maybe one or two have answered that they first learned about their pursuit in a school setting. It is my hope that some of the things that children can learn in music, as described in the pages that follow, are the sorts of things that people care about and pursue in their adult and out-of-school lives.

2

A Music Playground

Q: Do you like music?

A: This year we love it. It's wacko.

Q: What do you do in music?

A: Play games, mostly. And we sing songs, and compose.

Q: Do you think you learn anything from the games?

A: No, they're just fun.

Q: Well, let's take the Body Orchestra as an example. Do you learn anything from that?

A: No, it's just funny. Well...*maybe you do learn something about polyphony and texture and beats and how to watch for your part to come in and listening for your part with the other parts and getting louder and softer and stuff. And it helps when you're singing rounds. But mostly it's just fun.* [emphasis added]

Children's responses to questions from a visitor, March 1986

.... EVEN on the first day, working with the children was *fun*. Somehow the class felt different from other classrooms I had taught in before. Perhaps it was the lack of furniture and thus the lack of formality from the beginning that set a different scene. Perhaps it was due to the fact that we spent most of the time playing musical games. In any case, I described the music classroom at the Hennigan a few weeks later as a "playground" to colleagues, friends, and teachers. I used the term "playground" almost jokingly at first, as I watched children playing, having fun, giggling, talking, arguing, singing, and horsing around, just as children do in any playground in the park. I had no idea how fitting the description would become as I began to examine the playground features of the classroom more closely.

There are several criticisms that one encounters when it is suggested that classrooms or learning environments in general might be modeled after playgrounds. It is not uncommon to hear the following sorts of statements: "Children cannot *just* play at school. Play is fine alongside their serious work, but no real or significant learning can take place when children are only playing. Besides, where is the structure? How would we mark their work? You can't just let the kids run wild all the time." Even teachers who believe that there is learning in play still harbor doubts about dropping the carefully planned "scope and sequence curricula" (especially for mathematics and language), with the built-in "Good Housekeeping Seal of Approval" measures for ascertaining not only if the children have achieved the objectives, but if the teacher is properly doing his or her job. I will first consider the question of structure.

I have never had a desire to create a music playground without structure. Indeed, the playground in the park is a highly complex and highly structured setting in many ways. There is structure in the materials of the park. The swing set, the slides, the roundabout, the monkey bars, and the open, grassy spaces—all have structure and limits. So too do the piano, the beach balls, the computers, the paints, the costumes, the puppets, the cardboard boxes, and the open spaces of a music playground. But more important, there is structure in the way that the children approach the materials and the ways in which they interact with one another as they use those materials. Anyone watching a group of children play on the slide will quickly realize that the children will, sometimes with conflict but often not, work out a set of rules that they all more or less agree on and abide by. The same thing evolves after a surprisingly short time when a group of children cluster around the piano. In fact, I have found that these sorts of operational structures develop much more quickly and to the satisfaction of most children if I leave the children to themselves rather than presenting them with what I view as a fair, well thought out and detailed plan.

The materials and tools in a playground bear further discussion. In the music playground at Hennigan, and in playgrounds I have had a share in forming since, the materials and tools shared one important feature in that they carried with them no *single* implied use. Any of the materials and tools could be used to construct any number of things, and used by children with different skills and purposes. For instance, something as simple as a meter length of swimming pool vacuum hose was used as an instrument by swinging it around, as a device for demonstrating overtones, as an elephant's trunk, as a slide for a plasticine creature for an animation film, and as an amplifier for another instrument. Similarly, a tool like a hammer or a music composition program on the computer could be used to shape various products. Further, the materials and tools in the Hennigan music playground together formed a tool kit for arts creations, a kit that was enticing to the children and invited exploration and experimentation.

Because the materials and tools were so open-ended in nature (not just physically, as in the case of the hose!), and because there were so many of them, there was no need to have large numbers of each. In fact, a music (or arts) playground is one of the few types of settings where only two or three computers can be successfully used by thirty people because the computers are only one kind of tool, and a tool that can be used in combination with other tools of a similar nature. At the Hennigan playground, there was rarely a lineup at the computers or any unpleasant incident of a child feeling as if he or she missed an opportunity to play on the computer. The child could use other materials that were equally enjoyable and stimulating until a computer was available.

The materials in the music playground also cut across the traditional subject boundaries. While there were obvious materials for music making, such as a piano, a synthesizer, and Orff xylophones and metallophones, and obvious art materials such as plasticine, paper, and glue, it was natural for the various media to be used together to form integrated products. One group of children created an animated film using the plasticine to build their characters and the musical instruments as props for their creatures; later, the instruments were used to form the audio track for their film. Children who built cars and roller coasters out of Lego, while engaged in problems of motion and mathematics, were also concerned with the visual effect of their constructions, choosing colors, shapes, and forms to best represent their vision. Later, the child could take what he or she had built from Lego and write a LOGO

Playing with Lego/LOGO in an Arts Playground

program to have the Lego construction move, sense, and make new moves. Thus, the child was also learning about programming in a way that was embedded in play and in the constructions resulting from play. (Lego/LOGO is an ingenious combination of the Lego construction set and the computer programming language LOGO; see Appendix.) The materials in the park also share these features: in the best parks there are usually a large variety of aesthetically appealing materials that can be used by people of many ages, and in many ways. While it is true that slides are basically built for sliding, and swings for swinging, it is also true that children make their own uses of slides and swings—the slide is sometimes the cave where the bear is hiding, the swing is sometimes the rope of Tarzan.

So far I have mentioned the structure in materials and tools and the organization of groups of children using materials. What of intellectual structures? How are children to learn to pump on the swings, how to play the piano? This is a question that cannot be fully addressed in these pages. But what I will say now is this: children must be allowed to create their own ways of structuring the content of the discipline, and much of that structuring can happen through the manipulation of concrete objects—through play. It is ridiculous to think that every child will acquire the same knowledge, by the same method, and in the same order. Yet this is what a glance at most math workbooks and piano lesson books would imply. I have already stated that my favorite materials and tools are those with no single implied use or pedagogy; provide a group of children with bottle caps, shiny paper, hammer, wood, and nails, and just watch what they build. Provide children with a few "cognitive materials"—examples of symmetry, repetition, inversion—and just watch what they build. If the structure of the activity and materials are flexible enough to accommodate the content provided by the child, then the child will have the means and desire to construct his or her own intellectual structures. Playgrounds are not without structure. There is structure in the setting, the social interactions, and in the learning. And these structures are essential if the playground is going to work.

Another feature of these playgrounds is that children in such a setting have a communication network that makes Electronic Mail seem slow and ineffectual. If there is something worth knowing or seeing, you can be sure that in minutes every child on the playground will be privy to that delicious morsel of information. This network not only works for the news of the moment, but ties children together from one generation to the next. Somehow all of us learned the games of leap frog, hopscotch, the rhymes of jump rope, and the rules of marbles. None of us learned these games from the school curriculum. Few of us learned these games from adults. And yet, there is a common culture, a common knowledge of children's games. They were, quite simply, taught by children to other children by talking, showing, and doing. Talk, talk, talk, I say, and play, play, play! Why not show two or three children a routine on the piano? If it's worth knowing about the news will spread, and in a few days time, many more children will be playing than a single person, like a teacher, could possibly have taught on his or her own.

Should it appear that there are no tensions in the playground in the park or a playground in the classroom, let me stress that the playgrounds I describe are by no means conflict-free. But conflict need not necessarily be regarded as a bad thing. It is, at least, a sign of passion and personal investment, and can quite possibly lead to thinking and growth. When conflicts arose in the Hennigan music playground, I usually took on the role of a playground monitor. Minor skirmishes never drew my attention, especially if it appeared that they would be quickly resolved by the children themselves. I would intervene, however, when a conflict threatened to climax with a destructive explosion of wills, or where a conflict was disturbing to other children. But such conflicts were rare, and when they occurred they often became the focus for discussion and reflection. Most days, therefore, I found it unnecessary to assume the role of playground monitor. More of my time was spent as an activity leader. I often began a thirty-minute class with some sort of musical game (see Chapter 3) or an improvisation routine (see Chapter 6), followed by "free time," where children could use the materials as they wished, improvising and composing in the process (see Chapters 6 and 7). Sometimes, if children were having a problem with a particular concept (e.g., using eighth notes at the end of a long phrase where a quarter note should have been used), I would pull a small group of students aside and work with them for two or three minutes. Occasionally, perhaps once every three or four classes, I would spend fifteen or twenty minutes singing with the group. Most of my time, however, was spent as a player—a learner. I took great delight in playing and learning with the children. But it was not a hollow form of learning of the "Let's learn together" variety, learning something that the teacher obviously already knows. I learned along with the children, but on my level, interpreting and directing my own explorations based on what I had previously explored. This in turn modeled for them "real" learning as opposed to "school" learning, that is, the learning of things about which one has a real and passionate interest, not about things that the teacher deems worth learning.

I have used the word "learning" many times in the last few pages. Children *do* learn when they are playing, although they, like many adults, are sometimes dubious about learning and having fun at the same time. By the time I came in contact with the children at Hennigan, they had firm ideas of what "classrooms," "learning," and "school" were all about. One child asked me if I had ever taught in a classroom before, since I clearly had no idea, it seemed to her, what classrooms were supposed to look like:

> CHILD: Miss Upitis, don't take this wrong, or anything, but you know, you are a weird music teacher. Like you come up with weird ideas like collecting junk to express music ideas. Everyone else just teaches music, but you make us invent music. You could probably take two rocks and make music. . . . Have you ever taught music before?
> Miss U: Yup, for about twelve years.
> CHILD: You have? . . . In a *classroom*?

The children loved "weird" music so much that they were ready to protect me from the people they were afraid might ask me to change or leave. I remember one day in November when a fifth grader came running into the room to warn me that some authoritative dignitaries were visiting the school, with the unforgettable statement, "Miss U, there's four suits out there. I thought you better know." To give me time to get up from where I was sitting cross-legged on the floor and look "classroom-like," no doubt.

Believing that a playground like the one described is a powerful social and learning environment is something that many of us cannot understand until we have been a part of it ourselves. Some of my colleagues and undergraduate students express doubt about whether children would *really* learn anything, or at least anything important, in such a setting. Their views have gradually changed as they have spent more time playing and learning alongside the children. Similarly, some parents who drop by have expressed similar doubts. One parent came to pick up her eight-year-old son, and as soon as she came in the door, exclaimed, "Oh my God. It's madness in here. What a zoo." Twenty minutes later, as I watched her sitting on the floor playing with Lego/LOGO, she said to me, "Oh, this is so exciting. There's such a buzz of energy. And look at the amazing variety of things they're all doing." I am sure that her view changed because she became an active participant instead of a shocked and passive observer. The more that all of us are given opportunities to actively participate and take charge of our own learning, the more likely all of us will learn, and learn from each other. That children in a music playground felt that they could take charge of their learning was clearly indicated when I asked children if they would like to do one thing, and they chose another. For example, one child, when asked if he would like to try building something out of Lego/LOGO, quietly but firmly replied, "No, I'd rather play with the synthesizer." I doubt that he would have been as quick to make that statement in a traditional classroom. But by making that statement, it was obvious that he, and not I, was the one to direct his learning. Just as he, and not I, would choose whether to use the swing or the slide in the playground in the park.

The remainder of this book describes the games we played.

3

Music and Movement

CHILDREN love to move. Most days at the Hennigan they came flying into the room, running and skipping and looking for something interesting to do. I once taught a child who used to walk on his hands for the first few minutes— an enviable skill! I always felt that this movement—this sheer energy—should shape and guide their music making, just as music making shapes one's movements. And yet, what a monumental amount of this energy is wasted in telling children to "sit down," "keep quiet," and "stay still." Children love to move, want to move, and know *how* to move. There was never a day when children did not engage in movement in the music playground. I began most classes with a movement activity or game. This usually took about ten minutes, although sometimes, if the children were already skilled at the particular activity, we spent as little as three or four minutes on a movement sequence before turning to something else.

I included structured movement activities in each session with the children because I believe, along with countless others, that there is much to be learned through the body. Even the most simple movement games, like those I am about to describe, led to sophisticated and beautiful creations where movement not only illustrated a musical notion, but became an integral part of the expression of that notion.

The first movement game we played was chosen not because of its musical potential per se, but because I was looking for a way to learn the children's names by hearing and seeing them repeatedly, without appearing to do so. One of the introductory Dalcroze exercises I had once been taught seemed ideal: each child says his or her name while at the same time playing the name with a specified part of the body. Thus, if I were playing my name with my head, I might move it to the left and right for "Rena," followed by a circle for "Upitis." A child with the name "Nicky" might make a quick down and up motion with his head as he said his name. Immediately after each child performs his or her name, the group repeats the name, along with the movement. Once each member of the group plays his or her name and the group responds, we

The Names Game

travel around the room again, playing the names once more using a different part of the body. After playing names with the head, hands, shoulders, knees, feet, and elbows, there are usually very few names that I can't immediately recall! After all, I have not only heard the spoken names, but seen, heard, and felt them *performed as music.*

Even at this rather elementary level, the Names Game is a powerful one. I am sure that its success is due in large measure to the simple fact that people like to hear their names. And what could be better than having a room full of people play your name with precisely the interpretation suggested by you? Also, because the Names Game combines two things children know well—(1) how to move their bodies and (2) how to say (or play) their names—the children can safely create new forms of expression. Further, the best judges of how the names should sound and feel are the children themselves, not the teacher. One of the things we all know best is how our name is to be "played"—the tempo, the accent, the rhythm, and the intonation.

The Names Game at the Hennigan took a new direction when one child suggested that we play several names at the same time. Three contrasting names were selected, and the children divided themselves into three groups. Each group then practiced playing the name they had selected, including one or more of the movements designed for the name. I then conducted the three groups, much like one would conduct three sections of an orchestra. Thus, I could vary the mood and texture of the piece rather dramatically by two simple devices: bringing in and stopping one, two, or all three of the sections, and by varying the dynamic levels of each section or the entire group. When one of the children first conducted the Body Orchestra, as it came to be known, the expression on his face was one of pure disbelief. He kept glancing from the group to his hands and back again to the group, no doubt to see where the magic in his hands was coming from. What an experience it is to mold and create a piece from the musical material embedded in three names. This game also embodies a much more general lesson: complex structures can be constructed from the most simple elements. Only a few first names were used to begin building the Body Orchestra; only a few bricks are used to begin constructing a complex edifice.

As the year progressed, the children began to develop more sophisticated music through the Body Orchestra. Sometime in October, the children were asked to show what they had been doing

The Body Orchestra (Photo by Lise Motherwell)

in music at an Open House for Project Headlight. I was unable to
attend the Open House, but I had left some vague instructions
with the children, trusting that they would organize themselves
and replay some of their creations from class. Not so! We had been
using only single names in the Body Orchestra up until that time.
At the Open House, one child suggested that they try phrases for
each part, and so, the talking Body Orchestra was born. The in-
stigator of this new idea quickly gave each of the three groups a
part to say and left them to create an appropriate movement. I am
sure the parents were just as surprised as I would have been, had
I been present at the time, to hear their progeny chanting and
moving to "Cash or charge?," "MasterCard, Visa," and "Too much
money." The next morning when I saw the twinkle in the children's
eyes, I had a feeling that there was a new *IDEA* working its way
through the underground network. Sure enough, I was greeted
that day with a Body Orchestra song with these parts: "Hi, Miss
U," "How ya doin'?," and "What's up, Doc?" The Body Orchestra
was never the same again! The children had taken the original idea,
made it their own by choosing a subject (spending and charge

cards) I would never have thought to introduce, and then shaped the Body Orchestra into a structure that would come to communicate a variety of messages. As for the Names Game, the children had a structure—the Body Orchestra—into which they could "plug" their own content. This content is never the same from one group to the next, for the content and, indeed, sometimes the structures themselves come from personal choices based on culture and experience.

Yet another layer was added to the Body Orchestra when the sing-song chanting evolved to singing with instrumentation. One of the lovely phenomena of singing in groups is that people can almost instantaneously adjust their voices so that a room full of people sing in tune in seconds. If a hundred people are asked to sing the same note, within five or ten seconds the widely divergent first pitches become one. And so, when a group sings a name or a phrase, it not only becomes one within the group, but the groups themselves make reciprocating adjustments so that the entire Body Orchestra is singing in tune. Children can begin to safely play with pitches with their voices, and in listening to each other, improvise rich and unusual harmonies without ever having the teacher telling them which notes to sing. This is such a miraculous thing to me that I recently demonstrated it at a conference, hoping at the time that this phenomenon would occur for two hundred conference participants just as it had with twenty children. Singing three first names of people in the audience was quite beautiful—some people approached me later saying that they had tears in their eyes as they sang and listened.

One can imagine how the Body Orchestra became a vehicle for experimenting with all sorts of harmonic, melodic, and rhythmic structures, which were often later worked into children's individual compositions. Many compositions were created with nonsense words as well, where children were able to experiment with contrasting textures without concerning themselves with the text. One of the most popular parts for the nonsense Body Orchestra pieces was BEEP BEEP TWIDDLE TWIDDLE (see Figure 3–1), where the TWIDDLE TWIDDLE, sung an octave higher than the BEEP BEEP, was accompanied by the ridiculous gesture of a thumb in each ear with the rest of the fingers waving at the conductor and, should there be one, the audience.

The children became so fluent with the Body Orchestra as a form of music making that they were able to almost instantly make

FIGURE 3–1   *Example of a Nonsense Body Orchestra Piece in Three Parts*

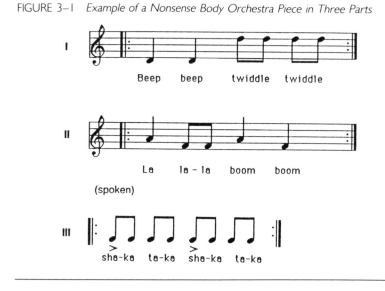

up a song, nonsense or otherwise, for any number of occasions. This was often to the delight of visitors, who would come into the room and be greeted with a personal hello, improvised and performed on the spot by twenty children (e.g., "How's life, George?," "Welcome to music," and "Stay with us a while"). What's in a name? Music, feeling, warmth, and power.

Sometimes movement games were far less structured. One of our favorites was to have someone play an instrument, often myself at the piano, while the children moved in any way they chose in response to the music. In watching their movements, I would frequently alter what I was playing in response to a particularly intriguing movement. Thus, the movement and music became partners in a dialogue, each influencing the other. Sometimes, what began as a soft and fluid piece developed and climaxed with a thundering crash. The same soft and fluid beginning might equally well end up as a tranquil flutter or a long sigh. In any case, it was neither the dancers nor the players leading; as in the Body Orchestra, where pitches were adjusted as every member of the group responded reciprocally, so too in the music-movement sequences, where the adjustments came from listening to and watching each other.

Movement Improvisation Using Scarves

The music-movement sequences were not always successful. At times they lacked the coherence, the flow, and the direction of the pieces I have just described. When the work was unpleasing, without form and flow, it was because the children and myself were unable to find or make meaning from the music and movement combinations. And without meaning, there was no emotional life in the piece—no music. Often when the movements weren't working, children would begin flailing their arms aimlessly, forgetting the significance of a flick of the wrist or the roll of a shoulder. When this happened, I usually tried to focus on particular parts of the body by asking children to move only their baby fingers or only their shoulders and wrists—a micro focus on what was happening. Then, when they once again seemed to be listening to their bodies, the music, and each other, the window could be refocused on its macro view of the movements.

The last movement game I describe in this chapter is an illustration of how, through movement, one can begin to hear music even when no music is playing. In fact, this game led to many a discussion about whether there was music in silence and silence in music. The game was simply this: make up movements for a canon or round, and then sing the canon with the movements.

Next, perform the canon with movements only—no singing. Finally, the singing was again combined with the movements, ending the sequence. All of this was done without a conductor, or rather, without a *single* conductor: every member of the chorus was in effect a conductor. These body canons were magical to watch— dancing, moving pieces of music. There was music in the singing, of course, but also in the movements by themselves. The movements carried the underlying beat, showed the phrases, played the melody, and interpreted the words of the canon. And then, when the singing resumed, the singing sounded richer—there's more to hear when one hears the sounds *and* the movements. Hearing movements without sound is a bit like tasting a recipe before cooking it: somehow the actual flavors are more intense after rolling them over in one's imagination. Sounds are similarly more intense after hearing them in movements.

There were countless other movement games invented and played by the children and by me over the course of the school year. A few are described in subsequent chapters, but many are not. Although I describe many more ideas in the chapters that follow, it is not my intent to provide a series of movement activities, or any other activities for that matter, for teachers to follow like directions on a road map. These activities would *never* work in the way that they have been described unless the children and the adults that they play with understand movement as a means of playing and learning, as an inseparable part of music, as an essential part of life. If these things are understood, then a manual of movement ideas is unnecessary and even unwelcome, because the ideas for movement generated by each unique group are the best ideas of all.

4

Trust and Risk

"We made up a song for you."

THERE is no trust without risk, and no risk without trust. Children continually risk and trust on the playground in the park, one spotting another as the latter tries to walk for the first time across the monkey bars. Although trust and risk are often less obvious in the classroom, it is essential that they coexist if any real learning is to take place.

In the first chapter, I claimed that one of the important changes in the school lives of these children was not brought on by the computers per se, but by the presence of the researchers in the school—caring people who wanted to understand the children, their lives in and out of school, their feelings, their thoughts. As the year progressed, it became clear to me that the role I was playing had less and less to do with the computer or even music, but more and more with my role as a person who was interacting with the children. While the things that we did together were based on music making, it was apparent that the experiences would not have been as rich as they were had we not together cultivated an atmosphere where it was safe to risk, safe to explore, safe to make mistakes, and safe to grow.

One often hears that teachers should "show themselves as learners" and "take risks in the classroom." I am particularly fond of one of Murray Schafer's (1975) maxims of teaching: "Teach on the verge of peril" (p. 2). But while I believe these statements to be true, I also believe that risking to learn along with children is a very difficult thing to do, despite the best of intentions. In my days as a private piano teacher, I had always wanted to take risks as a learner, but it was unclear how to go about doing that. At first, it was even less clear how to do that in a classroom, given the models of teaching with which I was most familiar. For most of my instruction had also been by traditional methods. Even if one believes, as I did, that those methods were often lacking, it was hard to know what to put in their place. And, although I had felt in recent years that I was learning "better methods," it was still hard to give up what I had believed to be right for so long. Sometimes the problem lies not so much in giving up what one has done, but in feeling that if a different approach is better, then what one has done for so long is somehow invalidated and wrong. However, if we have taught sensitively all along, and in so doing made changes in our practices, then surely none of the older practices were "wrong" at all, but part of the road to change.

"Trusting the children" involves more than allowing them to take risks in the classroom, or even showing oneself as a risk taker. It also means that one trusts that children will, given enough time and an environment that makes it possible, become engaged in meaningful activity without a great deal of direction on the part of the teacher. This is perhaps the most difficult lesson I had, and still have, to learn. A couple of years after my time at the Hennigan, I was working with a group of neighborhood children in an arts playground, similar to the one at the Hennigan School. The children were experimenting with fabric paint, making what seemed like hundreds of painted and splattered T-shirts, and using what seemed like thousands of dollars worth of fabric paint. I had to work hard to hide the part of me that occasionally wants to scream out and say such things as, "Why don't you try something different, something that requires less paint?" I kept telling myself that if I truly believed that children would direct their play in a meaningful way (as measured by adults and children), then if I just gave them enough time, a new activity would emerge.

A new activity *did* emerge only a day or two later, and it was one that I would never have thought to introduce. One child, for some reason that will remain unknown, suggested that four of them make a pillow in the shape of a watermelon wedge. After countless hours of measuring, estimating, imagining the stuffed shape, building models, painting the fabric to look like the fruit of a watermelon, and picking a fabric for the skin (green velvet), a beautiful watermelon pillow was constructed. The children then decided to make an orange slice, and the last I heard a kiwi fruit was planned. None of this would have happened had I intervened.

But it was, nevertheless, a difficult thing at the time to leave them to make their own choices about how to spend their time and use the open-ended materials of fabric and paint. Gradually, however, I am learning to give up more and more of the traditional trappings of classroom life. And as I give up more of those trappings, many more indications of trust on the part of the students begin to come to light.

One of the earliest and perhaps clearest indications of the trust established in the music playground at the Hennigan was the complete absence of vandalism or theft. At the beginning of the year, I was warned by my fellow teachers to "lock everything up—even the stapler." For the first two days I followed their advice. I spent well over half an hour at the beginning of the day and another half hour at the end of the day unlocking and then locking up all of the instruments, amplifiers and speakers for the computer programs, tape recorders, audiotapes, art materials, and so on. I despised doing this, not only because of the inherent message of *dis*trust, but because it was a colossal waste of my time. I calculated that, if I spent an hour a day locking away and setting up the equipment as I had been doing, I could spend up to 160 hours— four full working weeks—simply shuffling equipment around. I decided, then and there, to stop the practice I had come so close to establishing. It was worth the risk, on many levels, to leave everything set up all of the time. After the first few timid weeks, where I was conscious of watching to see if anything had grown legs and walked away, I thought little more about that decision to keep everything out and available; nothing had disappeared, and I had no reason to think that anything ever would. In fact, I gave the matter little thought at all until a visitor from England broached the subject once again, late in the school year.

Our English visitor, while impressed with the music made by the children, was puzzled by my apparent lack of concern over, as he put it, "the attractive instruments and other things" in the room. He asked, outright, whether I had experienced any problems with theft. I was pleased to report that no one had ever stolen anything from the room, nor, to my knowledge, had anything been taken from any of the children who came to play in the music room. Just as he was expressing his evident delight in this state of affairs, a child came running into the room, asking if I had seen his pencil. Apparently it was a very special pencil, with a sharp point and a good eraser. He had lost it during music, and he was sure that someone had taken it. We hunted high and low for the pencil. I was, needless to say, feeling rather sheepish as we were making our search, having just claimed that incidents of this sort simply did not occur in the music room. Just as we were about to give up, I remembered seeing the pencil, picking it up myself, and sure enough, when I looked in my bag, the pencil was there. As the child happily ran out of the room with his pencil in hand, I qualified my statement to the visitor, "Well, the only theft we seem to experience is by the teacher!" We then continued our discussion, speculating as to why there had been no incidents of theft in the music room. It was obvious to us both that the children knew that I trusted them to use the equipment well during our time together, and using the equipment well carried with it the implication that the equipment would be there for others to use at a later time. But perhaps more important was the observation made by the visitor that the children seemed to treat the music space as *theirs*, not as something belonging to the school or the teacher. Because the space and contents belonged to the children, there was no point in stealing what they already owned.

Children "owned" more than just the contents of the room. Partly because they felt that they owned the room, they also owned

Using the Computer for Composition: Musicland

the works that they produced. They were proud of their compo-sitions, as was indicated by their constant requests to somehow preserve their works. Early in October, a special needs child spent several hours writing a piece of music on the computer. After he finished his piece, he came to tell me, "Miss Upitis, I want to save the tune that I put." Similarly, children frequently asked if they could record their pieces, particularly if their melodies were created on conventional instruments such as Orff metallophones. Children often asked me to help them write out their melodies in standard notation, thereby fixing them in a form that others could also un-derstand. This element of ownership is essential if children are going to take risks in their learning and share and extend their understanding and joy of music. If they feel that the work they produce is theirs, and that it will remain theirs even with input from the teacher, then they are much more likely to experiment and create for themselves. Surely, there is much more to be gained in creating something for yourself than in creating something merely to incur the teacher's praise or approval, or to get a "good grade."

One of the features of a classroom where children have own-ership of their work is that the ideas for projects need not come from the teacher. While many of the compositions were shaped by my suggestions, it was also the case that children often came up with their own ideas far removed from the suggestions I had made, or would have made had they asked me for advice as they were developing their work. Two children, in preparing a 4H project, decided to talk about symphonies and rapping. Another group of children decided to write their own musical. One of these children came to me and described their idea, adding this statement: "Miss U, we might need you occasionally. Like if we need rehearsal time or help on the music for our play. If there's no one in the music room, can we use it if it's a matter of life and death?"

Perhaps the most important factor contributing to the atmo-sphere of trust in the music room was that I did not see myself as a teacher of *only* music. If music is important at all, then it is important because it is a part of life. Music enriches our lives. Music gives us a powerful way of interpreting our worlds. Music, just like any other subject if it is explored deeply enough, can offer the means of delving into any number of inquiries about mathematics, language, physics, history, and art. I view music as a means of teaching and learning about life, as a vehicle for making our lives more challenging, as a vehicle for making our lives fuller. The notion of music as an essential life force is in keeping with White-head's (1929) comments in *The Aims of Education,* where he states that "there is only one subject-matter for education, and that is Life in all its manifestations" (p. 6–7). A natural consequence of this view of curriculum, namely that the only valid curriculum is life itself, is that the teacher must be an honest member of the classroom in a way that is fundamentally a realization of his or her being. This means that the teacher must be perceived as a "real person" by the students, not as some person playing the part of "teacher" with the real person inside hidden from view. In fact, many children were not sure if I "really [was] a teacher." More than one child asked me, "Are you a kid or a teacher?" One evening I was invited to a child's home for dinner. The mother, at one point, stated, "This is the first time we've ever had a teacher over for dinner." The child who had invited me immediately and emphatically retorted, "Miss U is *not* a teacher. *She teaches, but she's not a teacher.*"

One of the reasons that these children were unsure about my role as a teacher was because in my time in the classroom, I almost always showed when I was happy or angry, tired or puzzled, or whatever else I might have been feeling, and I talked about and encouraged them to talk about things that were important. The time spent in the classroom was a part of the curriculum of life. As Herndon (1971) so aptly puts it:

> Time to live there in your classroom like a human being instead of playing some idiot role which everyone knows is an idiot role, time to see that teaching is connected with your life and with you as a human being, citizen, person, that you don't have to become something different like a Martian or an idiot for eight hours a day. Time to deal with serious concerns of the kids and time to deal with put-on concerns and time to fuck around and time to get mad either seriously or not seriously . . . but you can only live that kind of life in there if you are willing to realize that the dicta of the school are crazy but that at the same time the kid's life is connected to the school in complicated ways and you'd better offer him the chance to take any part of it he wants or has to. These dicta do not exist in themselves. *One is not Duchess one hundred yards from a carriage.* They too are part of what Dewey would call the continuum of existence. I prefer Wittgenstein's words—the stream of life. (p. 75)

For the children at the Hennigan School, their "real concerns" included things that I was only dimly aware of. I had no idea of what it was like to live in an inner-city environment, no idea of what it was like to live in a crowded housing project, no idea of what it was like to live with the constant threat of violence, no idea of what it was like to live without a father, no idea of the customs and culture contained in the music, literature, sport, and dress of many of the children I was teaching. Slowly, as they began to trust me, they shared pieces of their lives with me. Many of the incidents and conditions they described were appalling, not because I had never heard of such occurrences, but because these were children—people—I *knew*, people I was spending time with, people I was teaching. There are, I know, things I will never experience and understand that touch the lives of these children, or for that matter, any children. Likewise, even though I shared all that I could of my life, there are things that they too will never understand. But it was through these discussions that we came to know and trust each other.

One of the most touching indications of that trust was shown by three boys in their adaptation of a popular rap into what they called "The Upitis Jam." One of the boys approached me one day over the lunch hour to tell me that he and his friends had made up a song for me. I thought to myself that that was a lovely gesture on their part, never expecting anything more than a "cute" or "child-like" composition. I was stunned by their performance. They had created a fine piece, beginning with the playing of my last name, with one child chanting "Upitis [pause], Upitis [pause], Upitis, Upitis, Upi, Upi, Upitis," while the others "beat-boxed" a variety of accompanying sounds. As the rap unfolded, many statements were woven into a tight rhythmic structure. I was strongly taken by the content of many of these statements. One line, "Geography is one game she plays, one game people play every day," made it apparent that to these children music was not the only subject of exploration in Room 304. One line focused on the emphasis on original work ("She makes up all those rhymes inside her head"), another on my Canadian heritage ("In case you're wondering what all this means, she's funky fresh from Canada"). The rap ended with a dialogue between two of the three boys:

"We're not talkin' low."—"We're not talkin' high."
"We're not talkin' that."—"We're not talkin' this."
"But we talkin' 'bout Miss Upitis."

By writing a rap about me and for me, these children made me feel that they had trusted and accepted me not as a teacher, but as a person—a person with her own culture, feelings, thoughts, and ambitions, who could interact with them in a classroom setting, not as a "Martian" or "idiot" but as a human being.

To say that I was not a "Martian" or "idiot," and in some ways not even a "teacher," is to leave out part of the story. It was clear to me and to the children that although I could not be described by the conventional descriptors for "teacher," I did teach and my role was different from the roles played by the children. In some ways I was also their friend. In some ways I played the role of parent. Perhaps the best descriptor is that of "learned friend." By a learned friend I mean someone who can listen to the concerns of the children, but at the same time have an understanding about the world that the children do not, an understanding that includes not only a more developed understanding about people, but knowledge about some subject, like music. Part of my role, as I see it, is to teach something about that knowledge, largely through modeling. I spent a great deal of time modeling forms of behavior and showing my specific knowledge of music. For example, almost every morning I would come into the school early so that I could spend an hour or so playing the piano. Frequently, one or two children would come in to listen, perhaps asking a question or two, or come to the room to "hang out," working on their own music compositions or improvisations while I was playing. The reason that this form of modeling was so effective, however, was because I did not set out to model musical engagement, but was engaged in what I was doing. The modeling was not for the sake of modeling alone. I played the piano in the morning not to model that process, but because I enjoy playing the piano in the morning. This model, along with others like it, served as a strong model not because it was designed to be a model, but because it was something that I did for the sake of the doing itself, and nothing more. In fact, I would venture to say that all of the things we did in the music playground were done because they were good things to do in and of themselves, regardless of any future outcome of the activity. Engagement in things that are perceived as worthwhile, by children and teacher alike, whether they are discussions about things important in our lives, compositions, movement games, or playing an instrument, help create an atmosphere in which all of the participants can trust themselves and others, and risk to learn.

5

Performance

"Can you book me in for next
week's recess concert?"

····· IN many schools, performance is
the central feature of the music program. These performances take
on a variety of forms. Often the school music teacher conducts a
choir of "choice voices" (see Chapter 10), and the choir perfects a
repertoire to perform for parents. The choir may also mount performances outside the immediate school community, and perhaps
compete in the local music festival. If there is not such a choral
group or a similar instrumental group, then it could be that the
focal point of the music activities is a school musical or Christmas
Concert or Variety Show. In each case the emphasis is on *performance*, and this performance often entails the need for a formal
audience.

The role of performance at the Hennigan, and in my own
private teaching, is one of a much lower profile. This is not to say
that there were no performances of children's works at the Hennigan. On the contrary, there were many performances of various
kinds throughout the year, including a large musical production,
which I will discuss later in the chapter and then again in Chapter
8. It is natural for children and adults to want to perform music
that they have learned well or music that they have created. However, several features of the Hennigan performances made them
quite different from most traditional school music displays.

The most important type of performance at the Hennigan
School was the "Thursday Recess Concert." Nearly every Thursday, throughout the year, a rather informal concert was held during

the recess period just after lunch, from 1:05–1:20 P.M. These recess performances took place in Room 304, where there was a large carpeted area with no furniture, and where many of the instruments were housed. Thus, the setting was slightly more formal than performing only for one's classmates, but it did not have the formality of a performance on stage in an auditorium.

Every week, the program for the Recess Concert was posted in several locations and distributed to each classroom teacher. The programs were usually posted and distributed the day before, but sometimes during the morning of the concert. At the beginning of the year, I made the programs and kept track of the "bookings," but as the year progressed, the children took over this task almost entirely. The programs were produced on one of the computers in the school. This way, we could keep track of all of the performances, and children could easily make attractive programs and print them within a half hour. Besides informing the school population of the upcoming events, the programs served the important function of making the Recess Concerts "real." It was indisputably exciting, especially for children in the primary grades, to see one's name in print on the program.

These concerts featured a huge variety of works, including guest performances by vocalists, a French horn player, a cornet player, a 'cellist, several flautists, a guitarist, and a dulcimer player. Teachers and other adults in the school performed on recorders, sang, and played the piano. Children played recorders, Orff instruments, the piano, and flute, and sang, narrated, and performed their works on the computer. Some of the children played simple melodies that they had learned or created during their time in Room 304. A few, who took private music lessons outside the school, took advantage of the Recess Concerts to play some of their favorite pieces they had learned with their private music teachers or composed themselves.

The works that were performed also covered a wide spectrum. There were Italian arias; Mozart horn concerti; popular and traditional songs and canons (sung in English, Spanish, and French); contemporary works for Orff instruments, computers, and voice; Christmas carols; and ballads and spirituals. Many of the pieces were composed by Bach, Pergolesi, Beethoven, and other Baroque, Classical, and Romantic composers. Nearly half of the pieces, however, were composed by the children and myself. Some were improvised on the spot by the children and, sometimes with a leader, by the audience.

One of the reasons that works of Bach could be performed alongside the works of the children was that the children understood something of the composition process. In other words, the audience was an *informed* one. For this reason, each piece was listened to with gravity: the children and the teachers and other school staff in the audience had a good idea about the kinds of thoughts and decisions that the creation of each piece entailed. Also, a child one week might be a performer and/or a composer, and the next week might be a member of the audience. Therefore, the children gave each other their attention in a more serious way than might have been the case had only a few been "permitted" to perform while the rest were destined to be "only" audience.

The regularity of the performances was an important feature as well, since the children knew that every Thursday they could take part in a Recess Concert, either as audience or as performer (or both!). However, the children *were not required to attend* the concerts. Thus, there were a number of "concert-going patterns," just as there are outside of school. Some children never missed a Recess Concert, something like season's ticket holders who never miss a symphony performance. Some children came only if the program appealed to them, or if they were looking for something to do on a particular Thursday. This is much like my own concert-going pattern. I make a point of keeping free the days on which an interesting play or concert has been scheduled. Otherwise, I might check the newspaper if I find myself looking for something to do on a Friday or Saturday night.

There were also children who came only when it rained, and some who came only once, or not at all. There is nothing wrong with this. As long as children realized that the option existed, it is, to my mind, far better to allow them to make their own choice about coming. If any children were forced to come, they might never choose to come of their own free will at a later time, and this may well affect their interest in such events later in life.

Over the course of the year, the nature of the works performed at the Recess Concerts reflected the changing musical interests and abilities of the children (see Figures 5–1 through 5–4). In the first concert there were no children performing. The librarian, a fine mezzo-soprano, performed some classical and contemporary songs. Later in September some of the children began to perform, using Orff instruments and computers, but still relying on me either for accompaniment or sometimes simply for a little moral support (Figure 5–1). As children became more adept at improvisation, we

FIGURE 5–1   *Children's Early Compositions in Recess Concerts*

♫ **Recess Concert**
September 19. 1985
1:05 – 1:20 p.m.   ♩

Bells

Sally Cowan, metallophone
accompanied by Rena Upitis
(music composed by S. Cowan)

*Travelling Around
The World*

Orin Corey and Edgar Jones,
metallophone and computer
(composed by O. Corey and
E. Johnson)

Improvising on Breeze

Rosalie Chan, metallophone
Sandy Wong, metallophone
Rebecca Gleason, narrator
(composed by R. Chan and S. Wong)

T & N MIT Theme Song

Terry Tremblay, computer
Noel Little, computer
(recreated from a summer version
by T. Tremblay, N. Little, and
R. Upitis)

attempted improvisations with the audience participating. There were, of course, theme concerts, such as a Halloween concert (Figure 5–2). A larger variety of instrumentation and styles of composition began to emerge in November and December (Figure 5–3). The first concert in January was much like the first in September, with only two adult performers playing classical selections. Soon after, children featured prominently once again, and by the end of

FIGURE 5–2 *Example of a Theme Recess Concert (Halloween)*

the school year there was a consistent mix of children and adults performing contemporary and traditional pieces (Figure 5–4). This mix of composers ensured perhaps the most interesting Recess Concerts. It also served to legitimize the children's compositions.

FIGURE 5–3   *A Recess Concert by Children Alone*

♩ **THE TENTH SPECTACULAR RECESS EVENT!**

DECEMBER 5, 1985
1:05 p.m.

The Blood Song . . . . composed and performed on
Musicland by:

Tyler Billings

Little Drops of Water . . . . composed for metallophones
and performed by:

Jennifer MacDonald

Heart and Soul . . . . arranged for piano and
flute by:

Jennifer Price
Rosamund Scott

The Canoe Song . . . . led by:

Troy Brown	Harley Briggs
Guillamo Espero	Carl Miller
Bobby Thorndike	Delilah Oslung

Goodbye. . .Farewell . . . . audience!

After all, if their songs could be performed with Mozart's songs, then they must be, in some way, "real music." I understood this feeling when it was expressed to me by the children, for I too enjoy hearing my pieces performed alongside Mozart or Brahms in a similarly semiformal setting (four times a year I have an evening of music in my home).

FIGURE 5–4   *Contemporary and Traditional Works*

The Last Recess Concert of – 1986 –

···· Quintett for Horn, Violin, 2 Violas, Violoncello . . . but today, for Horn and Piano (faking it as vion, violas, and 'cello!)

by Wolfgang Amadeus Mozart   performed by Alistair Flynn and Rena Upitis

···· A more unusual "wind" instrument: Swimming Pool Vacuum hose . . .

The Adidas Rap for Hose and Voice

performed by Daniel Rees, Sean Shipley, and Terry Tremblay

···· Rondo for Garden Hose and Piano

by Leopold Mozart (obviously Wolfie was inspired by his mother, not his father!)

performed by Alistair Flynn (garden hose) and Rena Upitis (piano)

FIGURE 5–5 *Children's Canons Performed with Traditional Canons*

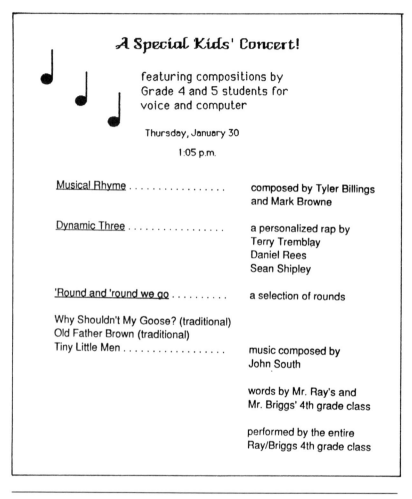

By the end of January, many of the children in the fourth and fifth grades were composing canons, and they often performed their rounds along with the more familiar traditional ones (see Figures 5–5 and 5–6). However, it is important to note that the children's rounds did not differ significantly in a musical way from those that we are accustomed to singing. They were different, however, in that they were more personal than traditional songs.

FIGURE 5–6 *A Canon Composed by a Child*

Tiny Little Men
Two-, Three-, or Four-Part Round;
Composed by a grade 4 student, J. Southwick
January 1986

Children often worked their own names into their songs, and certainly their own themes. Never have so many songs been written for aliens and green slimy blobs!

I spoke earlier of the importance of an informed audience. Since the audience was informed of the process involved in improvisation, composition, and performance, it was also a forgiving audience. For this reason, it was much easier to deal with the problem of nervousness before a performance. I overheard one child saying to another, "Just don't worry. Everybody out there knows what it's like, you know." This does not mean that children were never nervous, or that there weren't some less than perfect performances due to nervousness. But it does mean that the children were comfortable enough to try again if something did not go as well as they had expected. Having this setting for them to work out the problems of nerves also made for a much smoother performance of a large work, the year-end school musical.

Even though the audience was a forgiving one, it does not mean that we did not attempt to achieve some sort of satisfactory standard of performance. While I certainly did not require that every note be perfected or that every intended dynamic gesture be portrayed, I did ask that the performers (including myself and other adults) be sure that they had practiced their piece enough times that they were comfortable with the performance. Usually, that entailed playing it in front of only a few people first, possibly making some alterations, and then performing it at a Recess Concert. It was not unusual for children to ask to be "booked in" for one week, and then later say that they wouldn't be ready until the next week. I encouraged them to decide themselves when they felt ready to perform, and gave them the option of "backing out" and postponing their performance. Sometimes, but not often, this left us with a shorter concert. However, we never needed to cancel entirely—there were always a few children ready to fill in at the last minute.

One other form of performance, other than the Recess Concerts or large productions (see Chapter 8), warrants mention. It was not unusual for a child to be working on a composition during class, and at some point want to share that composition with his or her peers. One young girl, after working for several weeks on a piece for an Orff instrument, one day exclaimed, "Oh! I need an audience!" An audience of about ten people was quickly rounded up, made up of her fellow classmates and a couple of adults who happened to be standing near the music room door. She played her piece once, a few short comments were made, and then the people dispersed back to where they had been only a few moments before. Here there was nothing formal about the performance, but this kind of performance was also frequent and important. Children often asked for this type of audience and performance for works in progress and, again, the same principles of a forgiving and informed audience applied.

When the year-end musical was launched, it was produced against a rich background of performance. Children were already accustomed to playing, acting, and singing in front of an audience.

They composed their own music. They listened to and criticized the work of other composers, including works of Bach and Chopin and their fellow classmates and teacher. They knew how to use music to convey ideas, moods, and stories. Thus, they were ready to take a work written by and performed by others and shape it into something that they could relate to and tell in a convincing manner. In this setting, I feel that there is a strong place for a grand performance of some kind. But when major school performances are the *only* evidence of children's musical endeavors, or when one senses that they are in some way only attempted to please parents or to show that the school is concerned with the arts, then such performances are a travesty.

Performance is important. It is a natural outcome of wanting to share an artistic endeavor. But performance should never be the central or, worse yet, the only aspect of a music program. The performance is not the ultimate peak to climb. Rather, performances should be a series of footholds or markings along the road, as children and adults, alike and together, work at becoming better musicians.

6

Improvisation: Play First, Write Later

THE computer was not the only remarkable piece of technology in the music playground. One of the marvels of eighteenth- and nineteenth-century technology is the piano. The piano, like the computer, is a powerful tool for expression, for learning about form and structure, and for thinking about one's own thinking. But most important of all, the piano is an instrument that, with its pattern of shiny black and white keys, begs to be touched, to be played. Yet, what an enormous amount of energy many teachers and adults spend telling children *not* to play or, worse yet, yanking children's eager hands away from those enticing keys.

For the piano is indeed a magical thing. You press a key and instantly you have sound. A different key, a different sound. Touch it softly, and the sound is soft. Of *course* children want to play this instrument and explore its workings. And almost immediately after such playful exploration begins, they want to make the music sing from their fingertips.

Making music on the piano, it turns out, is not such a terribly difficult thing to achieve. It may take years to learn to play a Bach Invention or a Chopin Prelude, but it need not take years to learn to make one's own music, to improvise, to compose. When children find out that I play the piano, they invariably ask me to teach them how to play. I used to react to this request with a stifled groan, thinking, "How on earth can they possibly expect me to teach them how to play the piano in an instant, when it took me years to learn to play?" Years, perhaps (although not as many as I once thought), to play Mozart, but minutes to begin to improvise and grow musically through one's own constructions. I was a product of my training, and truly believed that to play the piano you first had to learn to read. Read first, play later. How absurd.

And so, when eighty eager nine- and ten-year-olds asked me to teach them to play, I took their request to be an overwhelming indication that playing the piano was something all of them wanted to do, and therefore somehow ought to be able to do. After a deep groan for old times' sake, I set forth to find ways to do just this: help a crowd of children learn to do something that they very much wanted to do—play the piano.

To play the piano almost immediately meant that I couldn't take the time to teach "skills" so that someday the children might be "ready" to make music. *They were already ready to make music.* We spend a great deal of time in music and in other disciplines "readying" children with "sub-skills" and "component skills," which often has the unfortunate effect of making them less ready than they were before, simply because their initial interest has been dulled. Thus, the improvisation ideas detailed in this chapter, including piano improvisation as well as more movement and singing games, as those described in Chapter 3, were not introduced to teach skills so that the children might make music at some vague time in the future, but so that they could make music, their own music, immediately.

The first thing we did with the piano was to use the black notes to convey a vast number of musical ideas. The black notes form one of the major pentatonic scales, a five-note scale that often produces music sounding distinctly Chinese or Japanese. The reasons for choosing the pentatonic scale were several. First, it is easy for children to "play the right notes"—any black key will do. Second, I could create the same pentatonic sound using the Melody Manipulations program on the computer, or by using a select series of tones on an Orff instrument. In fact, the Orff music teaching

Keyboard Improvisation Using the Pentatonic Scale

approach makes a great deal of use of the pentatonic scales, particularly with very young children, and often with considerable success.

What to do with the pentatonic scale? The first thing to do is to spend lots of time "just messing about" (Hawkins 1974; Koening 1973). Then children can do a number of things with pentatonic sounds. They can create different colors (black is usually slow, deep, and thick; pink is high and light), weather sounds (rain, sun, snow, thunder, lightning), sounds to portray different moods and emotions (anger, joy, sadness), and, less obvious perhaps, sounds to convey visual images such as shapes (circle, diamond, square). Children might be directed to try to have conversations with one another using the black notes, where one child plays a phrase, followed or answered by another. Sometimes the conversations are easygoing questions and answers, sometimes they are angry interchanges. Telephone conversations work on the pentatonic scale as well, where two roles and a context are specified (e.g., a mother talking with her daughter who is out late and doesn't want to come home).

These ideas of using music to convey moods, colors, and various other themes can also be extended to other scales on the keyboard. Besides using the pentatonic scale, children improvised

FIGURE 6–1   *Scales for Keyboard Improvisation*

Black note pentatonic

C minor blues

Whole tone

D major

D natural minor

Invented three-note scale

with the blues scale, whole tone scale, major and minor scales, and scales, often comprised of only three or four notes, of their own invention (see Figure 6–1).

One rich source of musical improvisation is to be found in the visual patterns that surround us. In any room, however barren, there are hundreds of patterns in the ceiling, floor, and walls, in the furniture, in the objects in the room, and on the clothes that people wear. "Playing Clothes" came to be one of our favorite ways to try new sounds for different colors. For example, if a child was wearing a yellow and black striped shirt with black pants, children would create sounds for yellow and black, using instruments and/or voice. Just as with the Body Orchestra described in Chapter 3, voiced sounds could be sung as nonsense syllables, real words, or non-pitched sounds. Once the sounds for yellow and black had been established, someone would then conduct the piece, using the clothes as the notation or score. The score could be conducted in any number of ways—horizontally, vertically, diagonally, or in circles; at any tempo; and with variations in dynamic levels. Sometimes there would be solo parts, such as the alternating stripes of black and yellow. Sometimes there would be a changing melody over an unchanging background or ostinato, such as where the fabric pattern was a series of flowers on a solid colored background. In any case, Playing Clothes afforded children the opportunity to experiment with sound for color, using the structure or pattern of the clothes. It also led to many a discussion about the importance of pattern, variety, and repetition, and so on, in creating a visual or musical form. Many such discussions were

Creating Improvisations by "Playing Clothes"

possible because children liked to have their clothes played again and again throughout the year.

After the first time we played this game, the combinations of clothes that the children wore to school the next day were dazzling in their variety of color and complexity of pattern. But long after the initial interest in Playing Clothes subsided, children would remark on other's clothes, sometimes playing them. Once they approached me with glints of mischief in their eyes, asking if they could play "the number" I was wearing. They proceeded to orchestrate the large magenta and white stripes of my sweater and skirt, and even played a variation on the magenta for my matching beads. When they reached the hem of the skirt I was about to clap, but found that they weren't quite finished. They also played my shoes (the kind that have no heel and are badly battered from days of school use), by chanting (descending minor third) "Boring, boring, boring, boring." I don't think I wore that pair of shoes again, except perhaps to mow the lawn.

Children also spent time building musical "machines," where each child was a moving part of the total machine, at the same time making a sound to represent the movement he or she was making. One or two children with an idea would begin the machine, and other children were free to join the machine when they had an idea of how they could connect with what had already been built.

Sometimes the machines sounded like a piece of factory equipment, where children would chug, whirl, and putter along with their rather stiff and robot-like movements. Sometimes they would form a creature, such as a prehistoric bird. Sometimes the children would build a machine with a distinct purpose, such as an automatic pencil sharpener or a train. A couple of years later, one of the children saw the musical *Cats* and reported with obvious delight how the actors had built a train during the scene for Shimbleshanks, the railway cat, "just like we used to do." As with Playing Clothes or any of the other improvisatory structures, Building Machines gave children precisely that, a structure for which they could invent their own content or purpose.

One improvisatory activity with voice that linked one class of children with another was the "Goodbye Song." This evolved quite by chance. At the end of one of the first classes in September, I sang "Goodbye" to the children as they were leaving. The next week, one of the children who had been in the class asked if we could sing the "Goodbye Song" again. I was puzzled about what

FIGURE 6–2   *The Goodbye Song*

she meant, but then remembered singing "Goodbye" the week before. I suggested that we add some more to the song, and one of the children suggested "Farewell, farewell." In this way, each class added their own line until the "Goodbye Song" was complete (see Figure 6–2), carrying with it the function of linking children from one class to another. Although this was the only song that we created in this manner, there is no reason why the same thing couldn't be done for other reasons, on other themes.

Another way to improvise with voice is to have the children sit in a circle, roughly divided into three groups. One group sings the bottom note of a major chord (see Figure 6–3). Another group sings the middle note, and the third, the top note. Thus, the class can create a major chord when singing together on some syllable such as "La." Then the group singing the bottom note moves down a semi-tone, the middle group moves down a tone, and the top group keeps singing the same note. When these two chords are played back and forth, the children are singing two different chords, the tonic or home chord (I) and the dominant or fifth chord (V) of the scale. The fourth chord (IV) can also be easily added. Beginning with the home or tonic chord, the group singing the lowest note keeps the same note, the middle-note singers move up a semi-tone, and the top singers move up a tone. The class can then sing the sequence I–V–I–IV many times, while each member of the class can improvise over the top of the chord structure. Usually the first time around I have the children take turns improvising, passing their turn along if they would rather not sing. After the children become skilled at this form of improvisation,

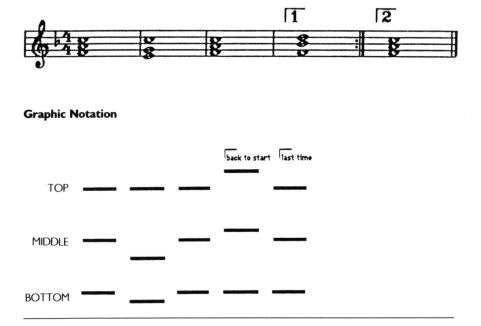

FIGURE 6–3 *Chords for Singing Improvisation*

Standard Notation (Major Chord Progression)

Graphic Notation

some beautiful melodies can be constructed by children in pairs, with one responding to the other, crafting a piece out of an imagined conversation. In order to play this improvisatory game, neither the children nor the teacher need to understand the formal theory around the chord structures described above. Children have no trouble following the graphic notation given in Figure 6–3 and, in fact, understand it very well if they have experimented with their own invented notational systems (see Chapter 7). This exercise can also be modified for singing in different keys, modes, and tempi.

The improvisations we tried were not limited to traditional instruments such as the piano or voice, or even the computer. Each time children encountered a new instrument or created one of their own (see Chapter 9), it was natural for them to "mess about" with the possibilities that the new instrument might bring. It was possible for the children to see, through the process of improvisation, that the musical elements of pitch, rhythm, and form were common to all instruments, regardless of type and origin. They started to listen extremely carefully while they were "messing about" to the sounds that instruments made. For example, Norman, when playing with the swimming pool vacuum hose, exclaimed: "That sounds like those bugle calls, and for a second there, it sounded like the 'Goodbye Song.' " He had, in fact, played a perfect fourth and a major third on the hose, the same two intervals that were used a number of times in the "Goodbye Song," and that are typical of bugle calls. And on another occasion, a few weeks later, Norman asked in excitement: "Hey, is the C on this thing [a soprano recorder] the same as the C on the piano?"

The conditions that I tried to set for helping children improvise, using some of the ideas that I remembered from my own experiences as a child in music classes, some that I learned along the way, and some that I created myself, all had one thing in common. In each case, the musical universe was limited, usually by the pitches that were specified, or by the idea that might be conveyed. However, again in each case, while the elements might be limited, the number of operations and nature of those operations were not. Thus, the child could create his or her own rules of operation, delineating how the notes of his or her scale (even if only three notes) were to work in relation to each other. More elaborate improvisations and compositions are likely to emerge when the child has first learned to manipulate only a few sounds, and later applies those manipulations to a larger musical universe. In any case, the children come to see music as something that can be used, like drawings and written text, to communicate and express messages, stories, ideas, and feelings.

One of the themes that runs through this book is that I was an active learning and playing member of the musical playground and community. Sometimes I found myself remembering the old adage "What's good for the goose is good for the gander," thinking that one might well say, "What's good for the students is good for the teacher." Nevertheless, sometimes it was just as difficult for me to explore new things as it was for the children. While I made different explorations from theirs, the process of trying something new and taking personal risks was similar. Thus, although I did very little improvisation with the pentatonic scale, I spent hours improvising on the blues scale. Playing blues was one of many new explorations for me, and one that I had never tried before my time at the Hennigan, holding the view that playing blues or jazz was something that I would never be able to do. Similarly, I couldn't imagine that I would ever improvise with my voice, bound as I was by my formal knowledge of harmony. These new ways of making music were extraordinarily difficult for me because I knew that I would make mistakes, unpleasant sounds, and that this would often happen in front of the children, or in front of my private piano students.

Other new ways of music making, such as using music as an expressive medium for nature, were less difficult for a number of reasons. For one, I felt that I was less bound by formal rules. Also, using the oboe to mimic the sound of a loon was something that I had thought about doing for a long time; it was more a matter of spending the time at it than avoiding it because I was afraid of the results. In all of these cases my improvisations, like those of the children, were by no means based on any new or revolutionary ideas, but they were new for us. One has to remember that for all of us, a new idea may as well be the first time the idea has ever shown up in history, for in fact, it is the first time in the sense of one's *personal* history.

One might well ask where such improvisations could lead. They may go no further than the moment, unrecorded and forgotten, at least in detail, but enjoyed during the process of their creation. They may, on the other hand, be important or interesting enough to recreate, edit, store, and share. In these cases, the process is one that I would call "composition." What makes it composition rather than improvisation is that the ideas generated in the improvisation are somehow fixed, and with that comes the possibility of future performance, change, and development. The following chapter describes something of this composition process.

7

Developing Notational Systems: Composition

"Hey, I don't need no C for this!"

Comment made by a child as he was selecting notes of a scale for a composition

"Miss U! I've discovered your secret. I know how you compose. You just put together patterns of notes."

························ ONE of the most frequent comments made by visitors throughout the year ran something like this: "What the kids are doing in here is terrific, but are they learning anything? Have any of them learned to read music, for instance?" When I answered that most of the children read treble clef notation quite fluently, the response was usually a mixture of surprise and relief. Along with the visitor's nodding head, I often imagined the unspoken thought: "Well, they must be learning something if they can *read* music!"

Although I believe that reading music is an extremely valuable skill and that all children should be given the *opportunity* to learn to read music, I am no longer so sure that reading music is as important as it is often made out to be. I have seen altogether too many youngsters give up on private music lessons because they couldn't read music, and therefore hated practicing what their teacher had assigned. I am convinced that teaching a child to identify a treble clef middle C at the first piano lesson, before the child has had time to play with the instrument, is a classic case of putting the cart before the horse. It would be unthinkable, in fact impossible, to read text before speaking the language. Yet in effect, this is what we do when we introduce the five lines of the staff before allowing and encouraging the child to spend a good long time exploring the vast richness of the instrument. One of the unfortunate results of the "read first, play later" model is that some people *never* learn to "play" their instrument, even after years of lessons and practice. By this I mean that unless they have a sheet of music in front of them or some memorized repertoire at their disposal, they are unable to play the instrument at all. We have all seen adults at parties approach a piano somewhat wistfully, saying that they used to take lessons. When asked if they might play something, all too often the response is that they "don't remember anything" or that they "can't play without some music." It seems tragic the number of years that many children spend learning to play an instrument, only to find that they never play again soon after they stop taking lessons. I am convinced that the reason that there are so many adults with years of private music lessons who never play their instrument is due to this phenomenon of read first—play later. Or, worse yet, play never.

I am also struck by the secondary role or even nonexistent role of notation in the case of blind musicians, musicians who use other forms to record and edit their compositions (such as audio recording devices or, now, computers), and musicians from other cultures who are able to play, improvise, compose, perform, and teach and learn new music, and never in their lives read a note of music.

Having said all of this, I nevertheless am constantly pleased with my own ability to read and write music. While it is true that part of my ability to read music is something of a natural consequence of my intensive classical training, it is also true that no matter how or why I learned to read, reading music is a source of much new learning and delight. Many an evening, I have had great pleasure reading through duets and trios with musician friends, sometimes working up a piece or two for an informal performance.

In a different vein, when I hear a new melody playing in the ear of my mind, it is a wonderful thing to be able to pick up a pencil and hastily sketch out the line or jot down a few notes. But in both of these cases, unlike most music reading experiences of children and, indeed, unlike most of the situations where I read music as a piano student, there is a real *need* for notation. In both cases, because I am able to read and write, I can experience music that would otherwise be difficult to play or remember. Although I could find, by ear and hand, a trio part if I had heard it many times, I am able to play a great deal of music more readily because I can read the notation used by the composer. Similarly, although I could remember a new tune if I repeated it many times, or sang it into a tape recorder, or sang it to someone else who had a better memory than mine, it is much easier for me to write the melody on paper. This is not to say that using notation is the only way to fix, learn, and manipulate music. It is to say, however, that music notation can be a powerful means to those ends.

How then can children learn a music notation system that would have the same value and fulfill the same kinds of musical functions as the standard notational system I know so well? Clearly, there is little use in teaching standard notation unless the children themselves perceive a need to learn the system. Children may well sit and listen to the lesson on notation when required to do so by the teacher, but were it not for the insistence of the teacher, would they do so? I suspect not. One of the most difficult lessons for me to learn has been that the need for a notational system, which would in fact make the teaching of notation an interesting and useful thing to students, may not arise for a long time—perhaps for several years. Sometimes I have wrongly rushed a child into learning standard music notation, partly, I am sure, as a result of my own training. For the first half of the school year at the Hennigan, the days where I would give some sort of instruction on notation were the only times that I insisted that all children take part and listen—a practice I abandoned some time in February and never took up again. It was difficult for me to accept that all children simply were not interested or ready for guidance on standard notation, but that when *and if* they developed a need for learning standard notation they would then learn to read and write music, and surely with greater ease and pleasure than would otherwise be the case.

The need to develop a notational system almost always develops when children compose their own music. It is this function of notation, as a means of recording one's own compositions, that compels children to learn notation, and forms the focus for the present chapter. Since the children at the Hennigan improvised and composed music on a daily, or at least weekly, basis, many children explored and developed notational systems. Simply stated, the children wanted to somehow preserve and share their compositions.

If the purpose of a notational system is to preserve a composition, then the notation needs to serve only that function. Consequently, many notations that the children used were not standard music notations, but invented to represent only those features of the melody that needed to be notated. Frequently, this meant that children would concentrate on representing pitch, forgetting about the rhythm of the piece. Further, they would often use symbols and systems for pitch that related to the instrument upon which the composition was developed or was to be played. For instance, on the Orff instruments, where letter names were engraved on each tone, the letter names were almost always used to represent pitch. By contrast, for piano-based melodies, children would often develop numeric systems, reflecting the groupings of two and three black notes on the piano keyboard. Thus, different notations were used for different instruments and, as I will show later, for different types of pieces and different purposes (see Figures 7–1 through 7–5 for examples of notations using various symbol systems from other domains).

I have countless more examples of children's notations for pieces written in a number of different keys and styles, including various scales used for improvisation, such as the pentatonic, blues, whole tone, dorian mode, major, and minor scales, and scales of the children's own invention. I would need to write another book in order to do justice in analyzing children's invented notations. I have reproduced here only a few examples to show something of the diversity and sophistication of the children's notations (see Figures 7–6 through 7–10).

Many of the notation examples reflected the suggestions I had made when children improvised, guiding choices about forms and scales. Some forms came from the children. In particular there were the raps. While I recognized the wealth of musical material in the raps, I made the mistake of trying to cram that form of music into the standard notation form that I knew best. It is simply not ap-

FIGURE 7–1   *Invented Notation Using Letter Names of Pitches*

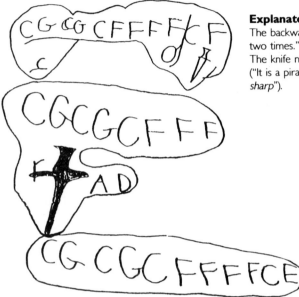

Explanatory Notes:
The backwards "2" means "with two hands and two times."
The knife next to the F indicates the note F#
("It is a pirate's knife, and a pirate's knife is *very sharp*").

FIGURE 7–2   *Invented Notation Using Numbers*

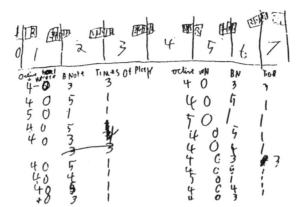

Standard Notation

propriate to try and write rap rhythms using dotted eighth notes and sixteenth notes! This also pointed to differences between myself and the children in how we process or make sense of new music. Typically, I make sense of new music and remember new music by looking at it in standard notational form. One morning, as I was trying in vain to notate the rhythm of one of the "beats" used by some of the rappers in the class, one of the children, in frustration with my obviously feeble attempts, grabbed the pencil, jotted down the rhythm, and in so doing, said, "Here's how it would go in your notes."

When children first have the need to fix a piece using notation, the notations are usually not very sophisticated or refined. This is not at all surprising, since they need only write down enough to remember the piece. The information they write tends to be pitch-related at first; rhythm is rarely notated at the beginning. Further,

FIGURE 7–3   *Invented Notation Using Icons*

con pedal

FIGURE 7–4 *Invented Notation Using Abstract Symbols*

Explanatory Notes:
This piece is notated with tear drops to show that it is
in a minor key. Other symbols are used as well, but it
is not possible to reproduce the piece from the
notation itself.

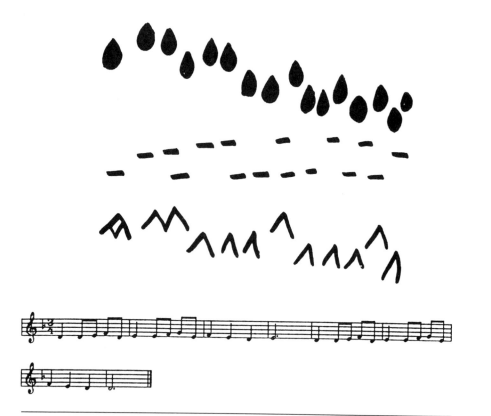

the musical information that they notate tends to be minimal; they
notate only enough to remember the piece, not enough to share it
with others.

Sometimes, after leaving a piece for a few weeks or after
someone else attempts to read from a child's notation, the need to
refine or develop the earlier notation arises. One child struggled
in just this way with a notation she had devised several weeks

FIGURE 7–5 *Invented Notation Using a Combination of Symbols*

Explanatory Notes:
This piece is written for black notes on a keyboard (pentatonic). It
starts on F#, and the numbers indicate the interval to the next note
(e.g., –I is down one black note). The curved marks indicate long
notes. The circled symbol reproduced here means "repeat as many
times as you want."

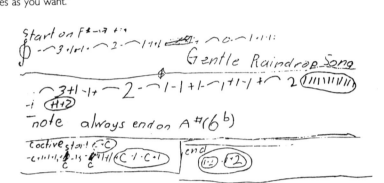

previously for a piece written for an Orff instrument. The notation
had no rhythm information encoded, and she tried the same
pitches in various rhythm combinations, commenting, "I'm trying
to see how I made the beat before."

Sometimes the notations that children develop become relatively sophisticated, and I often have quite a task learning to read
all of the notations so that I can play from their writing. At some

Writing a Melody for an Orff Metallophone

point there comes a broader need to standardize the notations amongst children, partly for this reason. However, this standardization need not mean that all of the children begin writing in traditional music notation. Standardization may simply mean that we all use the same system for encoding rhythm information—for instance, the same symbols for short and long notes.

FIGURE 7–6   *Notation Depicting Pitch Only*

FIGURE 7–7 *Notation Depicting Pitch and Rhythm*

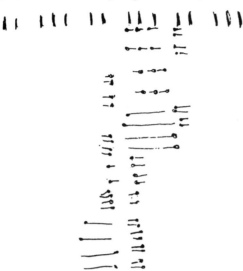

This piece begins as a familiar melody, followed by variations. Both pitch and rhythm are notated.

Standard Notation

Sometimes the need to revise a notation comes not from the difficulty in sharing compositions, but because a child's invented notation becomes too cumbersome in the attempt to notate an increasingly greater number of musical features. When this happened with one boy who had developed a way to show rhythm, pitch at various octaves, dynamics, and changes in tempo, I

FIGURE 7–8 *Notation Depicting Pitch and Octave Range*

Standard Notation

showed him how those features would be notated in standard notation. He embraced the system, saying, "I wonder who thought *that* one up!" How different from many children's attitudes towards standard notation.

However, even when children can see the beauty of a well-developed notational system, standard or otherwise, it does not mean that it is an easy thing to learn. Even John, who was so impressed with the standard notation system of sticks and blobs on lines and spaces, had a hard time learning to read it fluently. Occasionally during the year, I would work with a group of children on standard notation, using many of those competitive games to help disguise what was really a drill. I felt uncomfortable doing

FIGURE 7–9 *Notation Depicting Pitch, Rhythm, and Touch*

Panda Bear

Kangaroo

FIGURE 7–10 *A Standard Music Notation, with Letter Names*

Explanatory Notes:
The composer of this piece created a series of segments, sounding like beginnings, middles, and ends of pieces, using the piano keyboard. Then she assembled them in different patterns until she found a progression that she liked. The piece appears in standard notation in an edited form at right.

this, saying on the one hand that children would learn what matters through play, but knowing, on the other hand, that it might take a long time to learn standard notation, and that perhaps they never would. I still use drill techniques occasionally (flashcards, computer note naming games, team games like "SKUNK") to help children learn the notes of the treble and bass clefs. I believe this practice is justified by the fact that I do not play these games with children until they demonstrate a need for learning a notation. But perhaps it is not.

FIGURE 7–10 *Continued*

The computer played an important role in the composition process for children at the Hennigan, and continues to play a role for compositions produced by my private music students and for my own composing. It certainly had an effect in the development of traditional notational systems in that it provided a dynamic indicator of standard notation. Once, using the Musicland program, I had drawn a melody by gesturing a line on the Koala Pad. As the line was being converted into standard notation pitches, I made a prediction to this effect: "I think this one will be low sounds." After a Grade 1 child heard the piece, he exclaimed, "Hey! How you knowed that?" For that child, there could not have been a more appropriate moment for me to launch into an explanation of how pitches are spatially located on the staff. Another advantage of the computer was that it provided a link to other instruments. For many children, making original things on the computer was not difficult to imagine. After all, they had been using the computer as a tool for creating original stories, original drawings, and the like at other times in the school day. When I first suggested to a group of Grade 5 students that they might make up a song on the soprano recorders, using the notes B, A, and G, one of the kids asked, "Can you do that on *this* thing?" implying that composition on a computer was acceptable but that composition on a conventional instrument was another matter altogether. I have found with adult students that using the computer for improvisation and composition, or a synthesizer keyboard that isn't even connected to a computer, is sometimes easier than using a piano keyboard. Perhaps this has something to do with the notion that one is expected to know less about new technology than music, or that it is somehow more acceptable to make mistakes on a computer than on a piano.

The computer can be a useful tool not only at the beginning, but at different stages of children's development in composition. There is certainly little that equals the screech of delight from young Tiffany (Grade 1) when she first heard a piece she had composed on the computer: "Y'll look what I made! My first song! It goes wheeoweeeoweeeu." The computer is a valuable composition tool for a number of reasons, not the least of which is that it gives immediate feedback about the sound of the piece, which in turn gives the child the gratification and confidence to try other compositions, and on other tools. As children spent more time composing, they found that the computer offered the added advantage of making the editing process an easier one, just like a word processor makes the editing of written text a more pleasing task. As children become familiar with computer programs, they, as adult composers do, begin to exhibit preferences for one program over another. Even in the course of a few months, where there were two programs available on the Apple, some children came to consistently choose one program over the other, depending on the kind of music they wanted to create. One Grade 5 child, Tara, in commenting on her preference of Melody Manipulations over Musicland, stated: "I like the other one [Melody Manipulations] with real notes. The music out of this one [Musicland] sounds weird. You can't tell where the notes like F and A are going to be."

The ability to edit and manipulate a composition, whether or not it is fixed on a computer disk, also increases the possibility of children discovering, for themselves, some of the rules of Western harmony. One child discovered that he preferred intervals of thirds and sixths, and he wrote several compositions based on intervals (called "Place of Three," "Place of Four," and so on). Another child, Jennifer, spent some time editing the ending for a piece she had composed using Melody Manipulations. When she played it for me, she stated, "And I want you to know that the ending was *not* a coincidence." The piece, in fact, ended with a very strong statement of the tonic note (in the key of F, a G followed by a half-note F). Jennifer had used her knowledge of the tonic or home key, which she had acquired through years of listening to music, and was able to apply that knowledge by manipulating her piece, even though she was unable to formally articulate why that ending worked and was "not a coincidence." This is another example of using knowledge that has not been formalized, but can be formalized by the teacher *at that moment* when it makes sense to the child. Then there is also the distinct possibility of that knowledge generalizing to other instances when the child wants to create that particular form of ending. There were many other instances where the children understood a concept, but lacked the formal language to articulate it. When Terry exclaimed about his piece, "Oh! I love it. Miss Upitis, how do you raise the scale up?" he wanted to know how to transpose it to a higher key. Terry was already playing with the effects of transposition, instead of learning about transposition as some dry concept in order that he might use it at some later date.

One need not use computer tools to manipulate motifs in the ways described above. Children can learn how to use such transformations as transposition (moving the motif up or down by a fixed tonal distance), retrograde (playing the motif backwards), or inversion (playing the motif upside down), or any combination of these transformations (e.g., retrograde-inversion), simply by experimenting with a four- or five-note motif, which they have written out on a small piece of transparency plastic and can then twist

FIGURE 7–11 *Transforming Motifs*

The Original Motif

Transposition (moving the motif up or down a fixed
tonal distance)

as it appears on the transparency   in standard notation

Retrograde (backwards)

as it appears on the transparency   in standard notation

Inversion (upside down)

as it appears on the transparency   in standard notation

All of these transformations may also be combined (e.g., retrograde-inversion,
transposed up a third). Two other possible transformations are diminution (the
motif is played faster by some fixed amount) and augmentation (the motif is
played slower by some fixed amount).

and turn in any way on a table, or on an overhead projector if they
wish to share the motif with a group (see Figure 7–11). Once the
children have found pleasing manipulations of their original motif,
they can assemble the pieces into a composition, according to some
pattern. One example of a piece that was constructed in this way
is given in Figure 7–12, both in its original form and with the
notation corrected and an added accompaniment. The piece is titled
"Veronica's Pink Sweater," since the pattern (A A' B A A' C A A'

FIGURE 7–12 *Veronica's Pink Sweater*

This piece was based on the motif that appears in Figure 7–11. After Veronica had tried the various possible transformations, she picked the ones she liked and assembled them according to the pattern in her sweater. Her notation, along with standard notation with modifications to durations based on Veronica's performance of the piece, and an accompaniment, appear below.

Standard Notation with Accompaniment

A") was based on the stripes of her sweater (PINK PINK BLUE PINK PINK BEIGE PINK PINK PINK). This is an example of using notation not only to fix the piece in a reproducible form, but where the notation itself is manipulated to fashion the piece. It is interesting for children to see how these transformations are used by other composers. Examples abound, and in the Baroque literature, one can take nearly any Invention, Prelude, or Fugue by Bach and find examples of these transformations.

Despite the advantages of using standard notation, there are some shortcomings associated with its use. One of the unfortunate effects of recording one's compositions using a fixed notational form, whether it is fixed on a computer or on paper, is that this process sometimes limits the compositions of the children to what they are capable of notating. Thus, I have observed children creating improvisations that are rich in texture, melody, and harmony, but find that their notated compositions are relatively simple and less interesting. When this would happen at the Hennigan, I would, if I was in the vicinity, notate the improvisations for the child. Now, with the availability of synthesizers that can be interfaced with a computer, it is often a simple task to play the child's composition into the computer, and, with a few editorial changes, have it produced in standard notation form. Again, this is only satisfactory if standard notation is appropriate for the piece. If it is not, the child's invented notation may well be superior.

On the other side of the coin, sometimes the notation enables children to create better compositions than improvisations. This is often the case where the child works on a composition for some time, making changes and revisions to the original score. This is another task that the computer enables children to accomplish with relative ease. The Melody Manipulations program used by the Hennigan children had a useful editing facility, and it was frequently used by the children. Here is a portion of a conversation between two girls, who were working on a piece in D minor pentatonic:

"I think we put in too many rests."
"Yeah, and that last note—blip—should have been longer."
"Well, let's put it in edit."

Another advantage of fixed form over improvisation is that some relationships of form are highlighted for the children through the notational process. Issues such as closure, repetition, and symmetry seem to surface more often when children are engaged in the act of composition, examining their notation for the way it looks as well as the way that it sounds. They are more likely to make decisions about repeating a specified motif when composing than when improvising, and thus a more coherent form often emerges.

As for the other activities described in previous and subsequent chapters, composition gives children a way of making meaning and telling stories through music and, in so doing, relating music to other disciplines. One typical way of telling a story through music is to write a ballad. The children at Hennigan sometimes grouped together to write ballads, particularly if the thought of making up words for a number of verses was daunting. In one case, a Grade 4 class had been asked by their regular classroom teacher to write individual book reports on *The Cricket in Times Square*, a novel they had recently read as a class assignment. Faced, no doubt, with the somewhat dry assignment of yet another book report, one child came up with the idea of writing a ballad instead. The classroom teacher agreed, and "The Ballad of Chester Cricket" was created by the class (see Figure 7–13). They created the melody through voice, and after I transcribed their singing into notation, they wrote words for many verses. In the process, they argued here and there about which events were important enough to have a verse of their own and which characters had to be described. In fact, they were, as a group, making all of the decisions about character, plot, setting, and so on that one would hope they would make in writing book reports. The only difference was that this was a more enjoyable, cooperative, and later, a more public result. As they were asked to perform the ballad a number of times, they began to improvise different syncopated rhythms in the performance of it. With nearly each performance, the piece became more complex and interesting, as new layers of refrains and "boop, boop, boop, boop" accompaniments were added. With the exception of the piano and percussion accompaniments, they were all added without any prompting on my part. This is an instance of where the piece was a living, evolving work, as are the two examples that follow.

When children are engaged in the composition process, they come to see it as that—a process. One of the children's rounds, "Tiny Little Men" (see Chapter 5, Figure 5–6), which was learned and performed by many of the classes due to its popularity with the children, did not end as a composition chiseled out of stone. A few weeks later I heard four children, *not* including the original

FIGURE 7–13   *The Ballad of Chester Cricket*

CHORUS:

Chester Cricket came to Times Square
He met Harry, Tucker, and Mario there.
Mama Bellini didn't want him to stay,
But Papa Bellini wouldn't throw him
  away.

Chester Cricket arrived on a train
He came from Connecticut near a lane
All his friends didn't want him to go,
But Chester thought his friends didn't
  know.

CHORUS

When the Bellinis started out,
The Bellinis were poor and Mama would
  shout.
When Mario had the store it was a bore,
And when he found Chester, Mama was
  sore.

CHORUS

When Chester Cricket met Tucker Mouse,
In that little newsstand that wasn't a
  house,
They had just sat down and started to
  chat,
When he turned around and met Harry
  Cat.

CHORUS

composer, improvise on the melody on the piano, altering the pitches and rhythm in turn, and in the end, coming up with a new version. In fact, one of the most humorous examples of children's interpretation of composition as a never-ending process came when a nine-year-old, who was learning a Beethoven Sonatina outside of school, changed one of the cadences (in red ink!) because, she felt, "This could have been a better ending."

This related benefit of composing one's own music—that it gives one a richer understanding of the music composed by others—is similar to young authors developing a deeper understanding of the writing process through their own writing. One morning

Chester Cricket slept in a matchbox.
Tucker Mouse was as sly as a fox.
Luckily the matchbox wasn't too icky,
But anyway Chester wasn't picky.

CHORUS

Chester Cricket went to Mickey's for a
  drink.
He looked so sly he gave Mickey a wink.
Mickey gave Chester a soda to drink.
And Chester gave Mickey another wink.

CHORUS

Mario went to Chinatown in search of a
  cage.
He met Sai Fong at a very old age.
Sai Fong really liked his cricket,
He asked for a cage and he got it.

CHORUS

Tucker got some money for a bed.
"This is ridiculous," Chester said.
Tucker never felt this way before,
And all he wanted was more and more.

CHORUS

Chester dreamed that he tasted something funny,
And when he woke up he was eating
  some money.
He felt real sorry and he tried to find
  more,
But he couldn't find more so he went
  "bizzor."

CHORUS

When Chester Cricket ate that money
His best friend, Tucker, gave him more
  money.
But it turned out that, after all,
Tucker the mouse did not like it at all.

CHORUS

Chester and Mario went to Sai Fong's.
They had a Chinese meal, Mario learned to
  use "tongs,"
Sai had a very old friend at his   house,
Chester got leaves to show Tucker mouse.

CHORUS

Mario gave him some of his food,
But Chester fell in a bad mood.
Mario fed him mulberry leaves
Then he jumped with joy from his head to
  his knees.

CHORUS

They all thought Chester could start up a
  choir,
But Tucker and Chester ended up with a fire.
They all scurried around to put it out,
Before Mama Bellini came to shout.

CHORUS

Chester began to chirp for a crowd,
And everyone stopped to gather around.
Chester got very well known.
His music was in a very nice tone.

CHORUS

A fat man put his arm in Chester's cage.
Chester didn't know if he should shake with
  rage.
He thought the fat man had a horrible smell,
And he knew that smelly guy was stealing
  his bell.

CHORUS

Chester Cricket had to go,
Harry and Tucker were the only ones to
  know.
Tucker was so totally sad,
But Harry said that he should be glad.

CHORUS

when I was practicing a Haydn Sonata, Zapora, a Grade 5 student, appeared timidly at the door, saying, "I came to listen to the music." After I finished the Haydn, we looked at the notation together, looking for familiar symbols for pitch and duration, and terms indicating tempo. I played a few excerpts from some of the other Sonatas in the volume, at her request. Zapora's final comment about the Haydn Piano Sonatas was, "There's some good music in that book." There sure is.

I would like to stress at this point that in no way do I want to leave children with the impression that standard notation is the best way to record musical ideas, or that, as illustrated by the previous examples, once they are recorded in standard notation they are "finished." Standard notation provides a good way for recording certain kinds of music, for certain instruments. But many a composer has created, and not only during this century, a different notation that better conveys the musical intent of the work. The point is to create a notation that encodes the important information. No notation will encode it all. Even standard notation often falls short of delivering the intent of the composer, despite embellishments. We need to give children the opportunity to develop notations to represent what is important to them, and what cannot be assumed by a reader of the notation. When one is making a list for Thanksgiving dinner, there is no need to put "turkey" on the list, since rarely does anyone forget to buy the turkey. But cranberry sauce is frequently forgotten and, therefore, has a place on the list. Similarly, if a child has written a piece in strict and simple common (4/4) time, there is probably no need to encode rhythm information (the turkey). There is, however, a need to specially encode a triplet or the leap of an octave (the cranberry sauce). Thus, we should emphasize the need to notate enough to remember the piece, reproduce it, and possibly have others read it, rather than checking to see whether all of the various musical dimensions have been accounted for in the notation. Then, once the child has notated the work, it should continue to be regarded, even after performance, as something that might take a different shape at a future date.

8

Music and Story

When the creative urge seizes one—
at least, such is my experience—one
becomes creative in all directions at
once.

Henry Miller

The school itself shall be a genuine
form of active community life, instead of a place set apart in which to
learn lessons.

John Dewey

·································· IN this chapter I explore various
ways that dramatic expressions can be linked with musical expressions, one giving rise to the other as a new idea is developed. Many
of the activities I will describe are improvisatory in nature and
meant only for the class audience, or perhaps for a few others who
have also taken part in the process and thus are part of the music
community (see the discussion in Chapter 5 on informed audi-
ences). I will also describe how these activities can be enhanced
and practiced to form a prepared piece. Finally, the evolution of
the year-end school musical will be described, showing how the
first musical provided the setting for changes to occur in subsequent years. For it is this process of *change*, of telling new stories,
of telling old stories better, that is arguably the most important and
potentially creative growth, and one that contributes to establishing
a community of creators.

In Chapter 6, I talked about a host of ways that children could improvise with keyboard, voice, and with other traditional and some nontraditional instruments. One extension of such improvisations is to turn them into full-fledged compositions. This includes the development of notational systems to preserve the best of the improvisations, those that children view as interesting enough and developed enough to record for later use and sharing (see Chapter 7). Another extension is to apply the improvisatory skills in telling a tale. Here, children use improvised music either to illustrate a story or to generate a new story.

Using music to illustrate a story is not a new idea. Movie and television producers spend millions of dollars producing appropriate background music, theme music, music to build suspense, and so on, in order to enhance the stories they are telling. So too can children create music to enhance their stories. When children learn to illustrate with music, it becomes just as natural for them to use a keyboard to help tell their story as it is to use paints to illustrate a story visually.

When beginning to use music to illustrate a story, I often teach the children a few easy sequences on a keyboard so that they have some ready-made things that they can play. These ready-made sounds include "The Walk," a four-note sequence beginning on C and moving down the white notes (C, B, A, G; see Figure 8–1). "The Walk" can be varied to fit different creatures and movements: a high and fast walk might be a little girl scurrying home from school; a low and slow walk might be the father bear coming home to find that someone has sat in his chair. In either case, only the four notes need be used, but they can be varied in register, dynamics, touch, and tempo to form different effects. Similarly, "The Sinister Walk" (C, Bb, Ab, G) and the well-known "Moment of Suspense" sounds can elicit a number of moods and illustrate the actions and thoughts of a variety of characters. Sometimes, with children who have already improvised with the whole-tone scale (see Chapter 6), a "Fairy Godmother" sound might be used. In addition, any of the other improvisation techniques that the children have previously tried, such as making sounds of sunshine and rain and the colors of red and pink using the black notes (pentatonic), can also be readily incorporated for music illustrations.

Choosing a story to illustrate can sometimes be a difficult task, especially if the children feel that they need to learn a story, learn lines, and figure out how to act the story before they even begin

FIGURE 8–1 *Sounds for Story Telling and Creating*

The Walk

The Sinister Walk

Suspense

adding the music. For this reason, I often start with well-known stories, such as the fairy tales of Little Red Riding Hood and Snow White. I also suggest that the children mime the tale, using only actions and music to tell the story. Also, each actor only moves when he or she hears his or her music, and freezes when the theme music stops. In this way, the keyboard player(s) can control the action and affect the pacing of the story.

Normally, I give children only five or ten minutes to prepare. One of the reasons for such a short preparation time is that it eliminates the possibility of full rehearsal. After all, this exercise is intended to be improvisatory in nature, and the spontaneity of the improvisation is often lost if the children are given too much time to go over their actions and choice of music. Also, it means that they have to quickly decide on a story, on who will play what character, and on the theme music (or motif) for each character. Then, as the story is told, the embellishments are added: extra pentatonic improvisations to portray running and skipping through the forest, exaggerated expressions of dismay when the porridge is too hot, and immediate feedback and adjustment as the keyboard player(s) and actor(s) watch and support each other.

If there are several small groups of children creating musically driven fairy tales, then it is most appropriate for each group to perform their story for the others. Here the children are an informed audience because they too have taken part in the process. Also, it is fun for them to guess the fairy tale that is being enacted and to see how different groups interpret the same tale, should it happen that more than one group has chosen the same story. Because the fairy tales usually take only a couple of minutes each to perform, this activity can easily be done with twenty or more children within a half hour, provided that they have had practice at improvisation on the keyboard and have learned a few tricks to create suspense, lightheartedness, and so on.

It is true that fairy tales quickly lose their appeal. There are only so many fairy tales that children can portray, and children are often tired of using fairy tale material anyway. Also, many scholars and teachers have rightly criticized fairy tales for being sexist and portraying staunchly stereotypical situations and values. Children also voice these concerns. After each group had tried two or three fairy tales, one nine-year-old girl blurted out, "I want to try something else. I'm sick and tired of being the victim!" Her next story involved using the fairy tale characters in new roles: Little Red Riding Hood, Hansel, and Gretel came together to "finish off the wolves and witches once and for all."

The fairy tale example is one in which music is used to illustrate a well-known story. Another way of using music to illustrate is to have children mime, in a similar fashion, an improvised story. One way of doing this is to ask children to tell a "nature story." For example, the life cycle of a plant makes a lovely piece of improvised music and drama. First, the seed is planted, and then, with sun and rain, the seed begins to grow. When the plant has fully flowered, it produces seeds, which are dispersed by the wind, and once again the seed takes root and begins to grow. Here, the children begin to move away from the strict structure of the fairy tale, illustrating a simple story with music.

A completely different approach, but with a similar product, involves the use of music to *generate* rather than to illustrate a story. Here, the keyboard player(s) create distinctive motifs for a small number of characters, say three or four. When children feel that

Musical-Dramatic Improvisation (Photo by Lise Motherwell)

they could "be" one of those characters, they begin to move in accordance with their character. Then, if I am leading or present, I often ask, "Do you know who you are?" If not, the keyboard player and/or other instrumentalists play some more. If they do, then I ask if someone knows where the action is going to take place or around what object or event. When someone has an idea, the story is ready to unfold. I rarely ask the children to make explicit their characters or points of interest (e.g., "I am a detective" or "We are picking flowers"), either to me or to each other. This allows a number of different stories to emerge from a single set of characters and focal points.

When the characters have been developed and the point of interest and action has been established, it is then up to the players and actors to mutually engage in the process of creating the story and, in so doing, telling the story. Sometimes, if other children are watching, a number of different interpretations of the story are given. Also, the instrumentalists can shape the story in different ways, beginning with the same characters and conflict but resolving the conflict in a different way. Often, children are content to play with one set of characters for a long time, developing stories that are more and more interesting and believable. In this way, they also learn how to construct a story, finding that they need to introduce characters, establish a setting, and create an event or conflict with some sort of eventual resolution. However, they learn these elements of story structure through creation, not by memorizing the parts of a story in an English class. And it is through this type of creation that the story-making process becomes meaningful and can then be generalized to other settings.

I have not mentioned anything about the use of props or costumes in illustrating these musical-dramatic improvisations. There is, of course, a place for the added interest that costumes and props bring to the telling of a story. It is probably not surprising that those additions are often suggested by the children, and when they have a firm grasp on the improvisations, both musical and dramatic, then there is certainly a place for such additions. However, it is usually a mistake to introduce the "extras" too soon. Children are already familiar with using visual materials to enhance their works, and they often need some time to work with just the music and the acting so that they can become fluent with those expressions as well. When props are first introduced, it is common for children to overuse the materials, wanting a prop or backdrop for every detail. They soon realize that there are "just too many props to think about," and they will tend to cut down the number of props to a workable selection. Sometimes they decide to eliminate props altogether, returning to the original form, perhaps only adding one or two special props, effects, or costume pieces.

Once children have created a number of stories, fairy tales and others, in the manner described above, they often string together a whole series of tales and songs to create an original production. In Chapter 3, I described how children can sing rounds or canons using movement to enhance the music. Such rounds can also be neatly incorporated into a production of vignettes, where short stories are alternated with sung musical selections using movement and action. For example, the traditional round "Why Shouldn't My Goose" (see Figure 8–2) can readily be portrayed as an argument at the market. Singers, dressed in jeans and denim shirts, argue in canon with one another. Children in the junior grades (Grades 4–6) may select a number of stories and songs to perform for the younger children in their school.

Another way to use music to illustrate begins not with the story, but with some visual stimulus. For example, masks and

FIGURE 8–2   *"Why Shouldn't My Goose?" (Traditional Round)*

puppets, both of the commercial variety and those made by children, were used throughout the year to inspire musical-dramatic improvisations. When making masks and puppets, we first used simple materials—paper plates, magazines, and brown paper bags. Later, some children experimented with plaster of paris and fabric. Regardless of the complexity of the masks and puppets, most would elicit a mood or emotion that the children could then set to music, later making their mask or puppet a character in a story. As with the story and song production described above, these stories were often performed by the older children for the younger members of the school.

Other ideas for original productions are not necessarily driven by a story or a drama. When children have had experience in a number of improvisatory forms—using musical instruments, with movement, story telling, and so on—they are more than ready to produce such things as large movement sculptures (building on the ideas presented in Chapter 3) or music sculptures built from inanimate objects, or a combination of both.

It is important to also consider that telling a story through music need not be something that is meant to be performed. Sometimes children will use what they have learned through improvisation to tell stories from their life experiences, or to help them interpret an experience they have had or an emotion they have felt. I saw a very strong example of this during the

1988 Seoul Olympic Games. One of my young private piano students, a five-year-old boy named Danny, came to his lesson and said that he wanted to play "something [he] made up on the black notes." I said that would be fine, and sat down to listen. He played a very fast sequence of black keys, moving from low on the piano to the upper registers. Then he played a brilliant sounding, high and joyous section. He ended with a soft and almost solemn sequence made up of only a few low notes. When he finished playing he said, "That was the race that Ben Johnson was in, and when he won the gold medal, and how he felt when it was tooken away from him." Danny, in a very powerful way, has already learned to use the piano as an instrument to interpret and make meaning of his world.

In some ways, the other end of the spectrum of musical-dramatic performances was represented by the rather grand and large staging and performance of the musical *Mary Poppins*, during the 1985–86 school year. There were many things that made this school musical a special experience, not the least of which was that I had spent nearly an entire school year with the children playing, listening, improvising, composing, and performing. But of all the things that made the musical enjoyable to the children, it was probably that there was a sense and spirit of community in producing the play, a play that was described by children as "more like a *real* play than a school play."

> Well, like it puts kids together in a group, and I don't think a lot of kids including myself have ever done a big project like this in school. I mean, it's not like we go up in the auditorium and do our little thing and that's it.

I have often wondered why the classic school play seems to so often fall flat on its face. After hours and hours of rehearsal on the part of teachers and parents, it is all too frequently that one sees parents yawning in the audience and politely clapping when it is over, pleased that they have seen their child perform, but leaving the school auditorium somewhat short of elated. It seems that one of the problems is that these plays fail to create a sense of reality and community. This was probably not always the case. Some years ago I read a description, written around the turn of the twentieth century, of the school Christmas concert in a one-room schoolhouse. Here, the sense of community prevails over the entire description.

The Christmas concert was without a doubt the high point of the school year. Children and teacher worked on it all through the autumn. Mothers made costumes and supplied sheets for curtains. Fathers built a platform, brought in the tree, played Santa Claus. On the night of the Christmas concert the little schools sparkled with the lights from borrowed lanterns, the glow of the stove, and candles flickering on the tree. . . . All of the children took part, no one was ever left out, and there were always last-minute excitements, forgotten lines, torn costumes, stage fright. . . . During the autumn the whole community attended other parties to raise a few dollars to buy Christmas candy and oranges for the children. . . . The fund-raising parties were sometimes box socials, where the men bid on lunches packed by their ladies. Or they were pancake and amateur nights when the adults trotted out their songs and recitations for one another's amusement. . . . A surprising number of schools had pianos or organs, paid for like other extras, by money raised in the community. . . . Whatever the reason for a party at the schoolhouse, everyone went. The little children slept peacefully, covered by coats, on the desks that were pushed back against the wall. . . . Everyone made the most of the parties, but finally the time would come to collect your dishes and coffee urn, gather up the sleeping children and start home. If there wasn't a school barn, the horses were blanketed and tied to the fence posts all around the school. If it was a cold night, you weren't long getting home behind a horse who knew he was headed for a warm barn. (Cochrane 1981, pp. 84–85)

The community in the one-room schoolhouse, as in the Hennigan production of *Mary Poppins*, was a necessary part of the production, for without the help of members of the community, the production would not have been possible. Now, in our suburban schools with large populations and comparatively many teachers, the need for the community involvement in the old form is simply not there. However, that does not mean that such a community cannot be created.

Other things besides a sense of community made the production of *Mary Poppins* a special one. One of the things that made it real was simply the magnitude of the production. What with a cast of over a hundred children, detail on the props that included printing titles on the books lining the shelves near the fireplace (more detailing than was necessary), and multiple costume changes for some of the characters, the children felt that the production was "real" simply because we accorded so much importance to detail. When interviewed at the end of the year, one child had these thoughts:

Q: Do you think it was a good idea to do the play big? I mean with all the props and costumes.
A: Yes, yes, it was a *wonderful* idea. I liked the backgrounds the best. They were so realistic.
Q: What do you think it is about the big play that makes it so much fun?
A: You get the whole story. It's not fake.

Another feature of *Mary Poppins* that helped make the production "not fake" was that a number of children worked together with the help of a graduate student to make two short animated sequences that were projected on stage during the production. Children made hundreds of drawings on clear plastic cels, painted them, and then painstakingly filmed them, frame by frame, to form the animation film. The children involved learned a great deal about motion, animation, drawing, and painting:

I learned more about motion than anyone else in my class except Raquel [who also took part in the *Mary Poppins* animation]. In the unit [class unit on motion], it's just in general about what happens, but in animation everything has to be so precise, so you get real deep into it. . . . Because the animals moved when they were singing and so you had to, when it moves this way, then the mouth goes like this, or like this, or like this. And when you have more than one animal like Stan did, then if one animal goes this way, then another goes like this, and the other one you can hardly see the beaks [demonstrating the motions with her hands as she talks].

Subsequent productions, however, with far less elaborate sets and even larger and more varied cast in terms of age and school measured academic ability, still felt as "real" as *Mary Poppins*. Children argued back and forth about which production was better, deciding in the end that all were "good shows." Perhaps other features were more important than the fact that the children saw the costumes and props as being somehow realistic.

Both *Mary Poppins* and, later, *OZ* gave children a framework for interacting with their worlds. *Mary Poppins* was the more obscure of the two, for the story of *OZ*, including adaptations of the blues tunes used in the all-black production of *The Wiz*, had more obvious links with the everyday lives of these children. But even in *Mary Poppins* it was possible for children to identify with the story. Children were quite intrigued, for instance, with the notion that at one time women were unable to vote. Many talked about other unfair practices of society that are still in existence today. Even the penguins in the country scene were admired by the children, especially the boys who had perfected the art of rapping (see Chapter 4). Children were also fascinated with the language of *Mary Poppins* and with the Cockney accents that they heard when viewing the Walt Disney version. Many appropriated the language, using it in class and at home. The child who played Mr. Banks came into the music playground one day, proclaiming sternly, "What is the meaning of this unseemly hullabaloo?" Another day, I heard two children arguing about the longest English word:

"The longest word is antiestablishmentarianism."

"No it isn't. I know a longer word—Supercalifragilisticexpialidocious."

"That's not a word. It has to be a word that means something."

"It does mean something. Supercalifragilisticexpialidocious means very happy."

Children also felt, rightly so, that the production was in some sense owned by them and not by the teachers. From the beginning, they had a hand in choosing the cast. Children knew that when they tried out for a part they would be judged by teachers and fellow students, and not by one teacher or director "in charge." They also knew that as long as they tried out for a part, they would be given a part, even if it wasn't the part they had aspired to play. Thus, the process of casting the musical is one that is perceived by the children as fair and shared.

Children knew too that there was no forced involvement. Many commented on the importance of this feature. As one child put it, "If people were forced to do it, it wouldn't be the same."

The fact that all participation, even on the part of the teachers, was voluntary also made it possible for children and teachers who did not take part in the production to still feel that it was in some way theirs, since they were members of the school music community, if not participants in the musical. In a school closing speech, one child who had no direct involvement in the play at all said, "We had a school play called *Mary Poppins* that took a long time and a lot of work. It turned out to be a terrific play."

When the show was finally staged, it was heartwarming to see children helping each other get dressed, helping with makeup, putting on their own makeup, if necessary, and making sure that all supporting props were ready and that they all knew where each person should be for each scene and act. Teachers were also in the position of having to rely on the children's deeper knowledge of the workings of the production, particularly backstage. But these things were more than heartwarming, they were *necessary* if the production was to take place. Again, because of the magnitude of the effort, it was impossible for one person, or even a few people, to check on every detail. The community spirit evolved because it had to, just as in the one-room schoolhouse situation described earlier.

Even with the apparent success of *Mary Poppins,* at least in terms of the feelings of children and parents, many of the teachers were less enthusiastic. There was widespread concern that children's "important academic skills" would suffer, and that surely we would see a drop in standardized test scores at the end of the year since so much class time had been devoted to the staging of the play. It was extremely deflating to feel the thrill of the production along with the kids and then hear those sorts of comments. One suspects that the teachers who felt this strong concern about "skills" and "basics" (many of whom actively took part in the production) were the ones that one boy, Stan, referred to when asked about what he thought the teachers felt about *Mary Poppins.* Stan replied with some disgust, "I don't know what they thought. They probably thought it was EDUCATIONAL."

Fortunately, though no surprise to me, the test scores did not drop. The converse was true. But, nevertheless, many teachers saw this as a "stroke of luck" and still stated, "There will be no play next year. We just can't afford that kind of time."

I was therefore on tender territory when I suggested another production the following school year. In retrospect, I realize that I made a number of significant errors that first year. One mistake was the choice of script, or at least the length of the production that such a script entailed. I chose a story from *my* background and history, and although the children could use it to interpret their own lives, this was in spite of the story, not because the story was particularly appropriate to their lives. The following year we attempted an adaptation of two stories and scripts: the traditional *Wizard of Oz* with the relatively recent production of *The Wiz,* an updated version of the same story that was performed with an all-

Scene from a Hennigan Musical

Black cast. The adaptation, *OZ*, integrated something from both worlds. It turned out to be a much wiser choice. First, there was music that all the children enjoyed. Also, in the spirit of the adaptation, all of the adults involved were far more willing to have children change and improvise their lines, so that they were able to tell the story in their own way. One memorable example, from James who played the Scarecrow, were the words he incorporated from the fire routine he had learned at school. When the Wicked Witch set him on fire, he shouted, "STOP! DROP! and ROLL!" Needless to say, that line remained in the production and provided one of the funniest moments in the performance. In fact, all of the best parts of the performance were those in which the children had strongly influenced the choreography, the acting, or the specific words they spoke. It was a lesson to us all that the strongest aspects of the productions were those aspects that the children *owned*. The children came to see us as dispensable helpers, not as the leaders in charge. One child asked me, just before the second performance, if I was planning to come that evening!

In the year of *OZ* (1986–87), participation on the part of the children and teachers was again voluntary. As I mentioned earlier, the cast of *OZ* was even larger than that of *Mary Poppins*. As before, some teachers threw themselves into the props and choreography, some helped out on the nights of the performances, and some had no involvement at all. But there was a definite change during that year nonetheless. Since I was no longer living in Boston, it was necessary for the teachers to have a higher degree of involvement if the show was to take place. It was both during and after this second production that the earlier attitudes of some teachers began to change. Instead of saying that there should be no show the following year, the comments were more to the effect that we would somehow have to find a way to do it again.

By the third year, it was not only the children but also the teachers at the Hennigan School who had real ownership in the school musical. Partly by circumstance (I was in Africa for three months of the school year) and partly because of the growing experience of the teachers, my involvement was minor compared to the first year. The same teachers who had once spoken so negatively after *Mary Poppins* were now identifying the school musical as one of the most important vehicles of growth for the children, and an important way to bond members of the school community together. They made their own decisions about costumes, props, and choreography, seeking help with some of the music when they felt unable to rehearse or teach a particular song. Often, I was informed of decisions with statements like, "We decided to move the front dance line off the stage after the third song. Will you be able to make the music fit for that?" indicating that the teachers no longer felt that I needed to decide or even approve of changes in the plan.

After the third year, two teachers wrote a grant proposal to continue their work with the Hennigan musicals. They were awarded the grant and now are able to launch a musical on their own. Neither of them is a music teacher. Neither of them has any "formal" music background or training. But they have been involved in the process for so long that they have learned to delegate responsibility and find help when they need it, linking their growing expertise in visual art, choreography, and drama with the expertise of others in music. This is a major and important development. It is encouraging to me that such a change is possible. It is also not surprising that *real* change is hard work and takes a long time to accomplish. Weekend workshops on bringing music into school life simply cannot change teachers' and children's experiences significantly. As one ten-year-old commented at the end of the 1986 school year:

It's hard. Like, it's like, it's not like you just learn it [music] in a day and then go on to the next thing. But you gotta practice and keep on going. I learned that from the play, too. It gave us kids a chance to prove to *ourselves* that we can do something.

It gave "us adults" a chance to do the same.

9

Making
Instruments

ONE of the first songs we sang at the beginning of the year was based on an engaging poem by Shel Silverstein (1974) called "Hector the Collector" (see Figure 9–1). Hector collected junk of all kinds—bits of string, rusty bells, bent-up nails, paper bags, stopped-up horns, patched-up socks. Alas, when Hector shared his treasures with others, "all the silly sightless people came and looked and called it junk." Not surprisingly, the poem and song sparked a lot of discussion about things that children collected, how what was junk to one was not junk to another, and how one could go about using junk to make new things. I then asked the children to bring in "Hector-type junk" so that we could begin making musical instruments. Several large cardboard boxes labeled "treasure trunk" were placed by the door of the music room, and soon contributions of junk began to dribble in.

A few weeks later we started making instruments. I gave the children little guidance, letting them explore the materials and make their own decisions about how they would make use of the

FIGURE 9–1 *Hector the Collector*

Hector the Collector

Poem by Shel Silverstein;
Set to Music by Rena Upitis

HECTOR THE COLLECTOR

Hector the Collector
Collected bits of string,
Collected dolls with broken heads
And rusty bells that would not ring.
Pieces out of picture puzzles,
Bent-up nails and ice-cream sticks,
Twists of wires, worn-out tires,
Paper bags and broken bricks.
Old chipped vases, half shoelaces,
Gatlin' guns that wouldn't shoot,
Leaky boats that wouldn't float
And stopped-up horns that wouldn't toot.
Butter knives that had no handles,

Copper keys that fit no locks,
Rings that were too small for fingers,
Dried-up leaves and patched-up socks.
Worn-out belts that had no buckles,
'Lectric trains that had no tracks,
Airplane models, broken bottles,
Three-legged chairs and cups with cracks.
Hector the Collector
Loved these things with all his soul—
Loved them more than shining diamonds,
Loved them more than glistenin' gold.
Hector called to all the people,
"Come and share my treasure trunk!"
And all the silly sightless people
Came and looked . . . and called it junk.

visual, tactile, and sound properties of the "junk." I provided hammers and nails, glue and tape, and away they went.

I too built an instrument alongside the children. My reason for doing so was not because I wanted to model instrument making, but simply because I wanted to make an instrument. There is something undeniably satisfying about hammering bottle caps to a scrap of wood, decorating it with shiny paper and yarn, and then playing the tambourine for anyone who will interrupt their own work long enough to listen. Looking back on my involvement, I realize that my doing along with the children was important in several ways. For one, children had to rely on each other when they needed help in making their instruments (such as holding a piece of wood while someone else hammered something to it), because I simply was not available to do it for everyone. Like the children, I would help and be helped by my nearest neighbors, but I was not about to leave what I was doing to go and help a child in the next room look for a roll of masking tape. In fact, children rarely asked me to go and look for that roll of masking tape. It was clear to them that I was not there to serve as a helper, but engaged in building an instrument of my own. Also, I think that children were more creative in their use of materials than they would have been had I presented some finished instruments. One of my reasons for saying this is that I observed how many children made bottle cap tambourines after they had seen mine. A similar thing happened one day when we were making masks (see Chapter 8): I made a mask during one class and many children mimicked it in subsequent classes.

Another reason that their use of materials was perhaps more varied than it might have been otherwise was that I was absorbed in making my own instrument and didn't pay attention to what others were doing, and thereby didn't intervene. In one instance I would have definitely put a stop to what one child was doing had I noticed in time, which would have been a real loss for him, myself, and other members of the Hennigan musical community. Tyler was making a tambourine something like mine, but instead of using a short stick with multiple pairs of bottle caps, he chose a long piece of smooth finished wood and proceeded to meticulously wrap about half a roll of shiny black electrician's tape around it. Tyler then hammered two bottle caps to the end of the shiny black stick. When he first showed it to me, I immediately thought about the "wasted" wood and tape—the wood didn't need to be covered, and I hadn't meant for children to use the expensive electrician's tape in that way! But I held my tongue—I couldn't help but be melted by the big, full-toothed grin of pride on Tyler's face. Ironically, Tyler's instrument became a favorite of mine and of the other children. I would invariably choose it when I was reaching for a percussion instrument any time during the year. The instrument not only sounded good (mine, with its five pairs of bottle caps was often too loud), but it felt and looked good. The shaft was smooth to the touch, and the weight of it, because of its length, made the instrument satisfying to hold and to play.

The final reason why I believe that it is important for teachers to "do along" with the kids is that the activities we ask children to take part in should be activities that we would like to do ourselves. James Herndon, teacher and author of several books including *How to Survive in Your Native Land* (1971), from which the following quotation is taken, reflects at length on why the creative classroom projects he set up for children in an "open education spirit" were not of interest to the children when they were given the option of not participating. He notes that two of the irrefutable rules in most school settings are that (1) you have to go there and participate in the activities the teacher assigns and that (2) you will be marked on your efforts. When Herndon removed the first of these conditions, giving children the option of not doing anything at all and leaving the classroom altogether if they so wished, he got what he terms "a brief version of the truth" (p. 31). He writes that

all the great notions we had, all the ideas for things to do, all our apparatus for insuring a creative, industrious, happy, meaningful class didn't seem to excite the kids all that much. . . . On the edge of complete despair, Frank [a co-teacher] and I began to figure out what was wrong with the ideas that had worked so well in our regular classes. It was very simple. Why did the kids in regular class like to do all that inventive stuff? Why, only because it was better than the regular stuff. If you wrote a fake journal pretending to be Tutankhamen's favorite embalmer, it was better than reading the dull Text, answering Questions on ditto sheets, Discussing, making Reports, or taking Tests. Sure it was better—not only that but you knew the teacher liked it better for some insane reason which you didn't have to understand and you would get better grades for it than you were used to getting in Social Studies or English. (pp. 29–31)

Playing Glass Bottles (Photo by Lise Motherwell)

An Instrument Made by a Child

Having made these observations, Herndon and his colleague decided that the only way that meaningful interactions would occur in the classroom would be if the children were involved in a project that was of interest to them. Eventually, the kids started their own project, making a movie called *The Hawk.* At this point, Herndon states, everything changed:

> What was the difference between all the grand things we'd thought up for the kids to do and The Hawk? Why, merely that we didn't want to do any of the former ourselves and we did want to do the latter. Why should we have assumed that the kids would want to do a lot of stuff that we didn't want to do, wouldn't ever do of our own free will? It sounds nonsensical, put that way. Yet that is the assumption under which I operated, Frank operated, for many a year, under which almost all teachers operate, and it is idiotic. Does the math

teacher go home at night and do a few magic squares? Does the English teacher go home and analyze sentences? Does the reading teacher turn off the TV and drill herself on syllables and Reading Comprehension? Or do any of us do any of those things, even in the classroom? (pp. 44–45)

But the music teacher, at least this one, *does* go home at night and make instruments, *does* go home at night and play the piano, *does* go home at night and work on a composition, *does* go home at night and do lots of other things that I do and have kids do in the classroom. I do these things and many others just because I enjoy doing them. I don't explore new instrument sounds because I think I will learn something about acoustics. I do it because it's fun. And I do it when I feel like doing it—not once a year during the "instrument-making unit." Similarly, instrument making at the Hennigan did not end with the bottle cap shakers and tambourines in October. Children made instruments throughout the year. Sometimes they would make instruments because some new addition to the junk pile was intriguing. (Once, after I had visited the Boston Children's Museum and returned with a few shopping bags full of materials like foam, plastic tubes, paper, and cardboard of various shapes, colors, and sizes, there was a predictable rash of instrument making using the most enticing of these materials.) Sometimes they would make instruments because they wanted to create a particular sound for one of their compositions or to accompany a song or piece performed on another instrument. Sometimes they would make instruments because that's what they felt like doing that day in music class. Sometimes they would make instruments because I had provided a particular focus for making instruments, as with the first "Hector the Collector" experience. And sometimes they would make instruments because they didn't feel like doing anything else. One of the important lessons I learned through instrument making, which extended to other areas of music participation, was that all of the children did not have to be doing the same thing at the same time. In fact, if some children over the course of the entire school year *never* chose to make an instrument, that too was completely acceptable.

One of the instrument-making sessions that I planned as an activity for those children who chose to participate was inspired by my own recent discovery about stringed instruments. A friend was visiting from Kingston, Ontario, and she brought with her a 'cello and a superb idea for playing with string sounds. Before

Playing String

playing her 'cello, all of us took strings of various lengths and thicknesses and "played" them in the following fashion. If you wrap one end of a piece of string (eight to sixteen inches long) two or three times around an index finger, then put that index finger near or in your ear, holding the other end of the string with the other hand, and then pluck the string with one of the remaining fingers of either hand, a very distinct string-like sound can be heard—but only by the player. This very private instrument (given the name "buitar" by one of the children) has all of the features of a stringed instrument. Pitch can be varied in three ways—by changing the length of the string (like putting fingers on the neck of a stringed instrument), by changing the tension of the string (like turning the pegs to tune the strings), or by changing the string itself to a thicker or thinner one (strings on violins and guitars range in thickness; thicker strings are used for the lower pitches). Predictably, the children were absorbed in experimenting with the different strings for some time, and they would often use a piece of string months later either to test some private theory or just for the fun of playing the instrument. Many, of course, wanted others to hear what they were playing, which led to a discussion of amplification and the role of the shapely wooden body of the 'cello.

Later, when some of the children decided to make "public" stringed instruments, their understanding of how to make different pitches and how to amplify them was considerable.

Because the strings activity, like the woodwind explorations with straws that I am about to describe, were in a sense "teacher directed," it does not mean that the activities took on the deadly nature described earlier by Herndon, that is, better than the "regular stuff" but still not exciting. There were at least four reasons for this. For starters, the kids, I am sure, could sense my excitement with the ideas. I often heard sentiments to the effect, "Oh, oh. Miss U looks excited. I bet she has an IDEA. We better lock her up in a closet!" Second, I explored along with the children, again not because I wanted to model the act of exploration but because I hadn't (and still haven't) finished exploring with string and straws. Third, the children always had the option of not participating. If they were not interested in what the rest of us were doing, then they could go off and make music some other way or work on some other project. Along the same vein, the string playing only continued for as long as each child was interested in the activity. When their interest subsided, they could go on and do

Cutting Straws (Photo by Lise Motherwell)

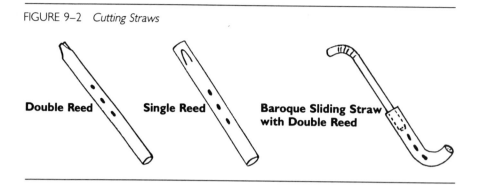

FIGURE 9–2 *Cutting Straws*

Double Reed **Single Reed** **Baroque Sliding Straw with Double Reed**

something else, regardless of what the other members of the class were doing. Finally, the children knew that they were not going to be marked on how well they played a piece of string or understood some notions of acoustics.

Playing straws, another marvelous idea for exploring sound, was introduced to me a few years back by a new acquaintance from San Francisco. One day when we were having lunch at the conference where we had met the day before, she surprised me and all of the people within earshot by taking her drinking straw, chopping a few holes in it (with a pair of scissors she wears around her neck like some people wear a pen or a necklace!), and playing some simple tune like "Mary Had a Little Lamb." Of course everyone was intrigued by the performance. She then proceeded to make a huge variety of sounds and instruments using straws, including single and double reed instruments, instruments with holes, and slide instruments (by using two straws of different sizes; see Figure 9–2). Playing straws, or "plasticwinds" as they came to be called by the kids at the Hennigan, was just as delightful at school as at that conference lunch. Of course the children went far beyond the original ideas I gave them. One child made an instrument thirty-two straws long, the longest plasticwind possible where a sound could still be heard (a bit like the "putt, putt" of a dying lawn-mower, but a sound nonetheless). Another child taught himself to play two instruments at the same time, one out of the left and one out of the right side of his mouth. By this time I had already learned to let kids make what they wanted out of the experience I had set up for them initially, so instead of feeling as I did with the electrician's tape tambourine, I was thrilled to see the new uses for

Playing Two Straws at Once (Photo by Lise Motherwell)

straws and other tubes that they invented. It was with a sense of considerable sadness, therefore, that I listened some time later about how one teacher had adopted the plasticwinds idea for her own classroom. After giving a "teacher demonstration," she handed pre-cut straws to the children, since, as she put it, if the children cut their own straws "they might get the pitches wrong."

Another music maker that should find a place in every home and classroom is the swimming pool vacuum hose. (Imagine the strange looks I received when, in the middle of the winter, I visited the neighborhood Pool and Patio shop and asked for thirty meters of pool vacuum hose.) If you take a length of at least a meter and whip the hose around at various speeds, different notes will play corresponding to the different frequencies created by the speed of spinning. In fact, the notes form some sort of overtone series for the fundamental note, which is determined by the length of the hose. If several people play several hoses, a rather chilling choral effect can be created. Of course, as with all of the other materials used by the children, they found new ways of playing hose as well. One child took the mouthpiece off of an old-fashioned bicycle horn and made the hose into a brassy sounding instrument (a new breed is perhaps in the offing . . . the "plasticbrasses"?). Another child used the tube as an amplifier for beat-boxing.

If "plasticwinds" and "plasticbrasses," why not "glass-winds"? There is nothing new about filling jars with water at different levels and making pitched instruments—each jar produces a different pitch when hit with a stick. There was a great deal of water spilled over precisely such "glasswinds" over the course of the year. But now, my own explorations had become richer, more intense, and more varied because of what I was learning from the children. A case in point was during the month of April when I was vacationing on St. Kitts, a small island in the West Indies. One of the reasons why St. Kitts is such a popular holiday spot is that the trade winds moderate the temperature throughout the year. One afternoon, as I was lazily lounging by the pool sipping on a bottle of beer, those trade winds started to play my beer bottle. This was much like blowing over the lip of a pop bottle, except that because the wind was so strong and steady, it was doing the playing for me. Quickly I ordered five or six more bottles of beer, planning to drink the bottles down to various levels to make chords. While I was playing around with the chords, I started to develop a technique for silencing the notes I didn't want to hear, simply by plugging the top of the bottle with one of my fingers. After quite a little while (it started to get dark, and it doesn't get dark very early in that part of the world), I was able to play melodies on my "instrument," sometimes with harmonic accompaniment. In the end, the notes all became one as the bottles were gradually emptied. I have never looked at a bottle of beer in quite the same way since.

When children make instruments such as those I have described, they tend to be less inhibited about making up sounds on their newly made instruments than they do on traditional instruments. This is partly true, I am sure, because many classroom-made or homemade instruments are percussive in nature, and therefore easier to experiment with and to play. It is also true, I think, because children sometimes don't think of their own instruments as "real," and therefore there is no "real" or "proper" way to play them, either.

In order for children to learn to improvise and compose just as naturally on traditional instruments as on others, at least two conditions need to be set. One is that the instruments that the children have made need to be legitimized, somehow made "real." Then, if they can improvise on their instruments, the argument goes, they can also improvise on conventional "real" instruments. One way of doing this is simply to *use* the instruments that the children have fashioned along with the instruments that they recognize as, in some way, already "real." I have observed many teachers spend countless hours crafting lovely instruments with children, only to find that the instruments either stay in a box for the remainder of the year or the children take their treasures home without ever getting a chance to explore their instruments fully at school.

Another way of making the instruments real is to show children how traditional instruments have been used in new ways. Children and adults alike often find it hard to believe that a famous composer like John Cage would roll a golf ball across the strings of a grand piano as part of a composition. However, once they start to think about new ways to play old instruments, and the new forms of music that new ways of playing create, they start to see how their own instruments have a place in that process.

There is often an enhanced appreciation of conventional instruments after children have had considerable time to explore and make various instruments themselves, particularly if they can see that there is some relationship between their instruments and conventional ones. At one point during the year, a visitor from Zimbabwe came and played various African instruments. One was the mbira. The mbira, sometimes called a thumb piano, is a series of strips of metal arranged over a hollow chamber, such as a coconut or carved bowl of wood. The mbira we saw had several bottle caps nailed into the bottom of the chamber, which gave the mbira its distinctively raspy timbre. One child exclaimed in surprise, "Hey, Miss U, someone besides you uses bottle caps for making instruments!"

Similarly, during one of the recess concerts, a resident musician played not only his French horn but also an excerpt from Handel's Water Music on an old piece of garden hose, using a French horn mouthpiece. While it was certainly amusing to hear the Water Music spewing forth from the hose, it was also clear that the children understood how the sound was produced in each case. One child even stated, "Making instruments isn't all that hard. All you need to know is how they work." While it is true that one need not know how to construct a piano in order to play one, just as one need not know how to build a car in order to drive one, it is also true that one's playing is often more imaginative if something about the fundamental nature of the instrument is understood. I am sure that the best way to learn something about instruments is to make them, manipulating some of the variables that make one instrument different from the next.

10

Johnny Monotone

ONE of the most poignant lessons I learned during my year at Hennigan was about "tone deafness." I put tone deafness in quotation marks because I am becoming less and less sure about the existence of such a phenomenon. I certainly doubt that tone deafness exists in the almost epidemic proportions one hears about.

We have all heard children and adults fail to produce the tones they try to sing. But "deafness" means not being able to hear. If that were the case, then two conclusions would necessarily follow. First, people who were tone deaf would not be able to hear the difference between their singing and the accurately pitched singing of others. This is often simply not true. As one of my adult colleagues once put it, "I know when I'm off. I can hear it. I just don't know how to sing the right notes." The second conclusion one is likely to draw is this: once tone deaf, always tone deaf. The argument I propose here is that the problem, for some people at least, may not be the inability to hear but the inability to produce.

Let me venture one step further and say that given appropriate social and musical circumstances, pitch production can be learned.

Early in the fall of 1985 a choir was formed at the Hennigan School. Children joined if they wanted to sing—there were no auditions and no scheduled performances. (They sang once at Christmas at the request of other teachers in the school.) In the group of some seventy children who came to sing, there were four boys who stood out for several reasons. For starters, they were the tallest and the most physically mature boys in the school. They were also ringleaders—popular, well-liked, and the perpetrators and organizers of much of the underground school action. I was surprised and pleased to see them join the choir. I suspect that their reasons for doing so were mixed: many of the popular girls had also joined; the boys had liked their music experiences in and around Room 304 and wanted more of the same; they were enticed by the social benefits of interacting with a group of friends and peers; and, perhaps, they wanted to sing.

By our second or third meeting something became blatantly obvious to a few of the girls with crystal clear voices, who could readily produce notes exactly on pitch. To put it bluntly, the four boys were singing boldly and confidently in an unpleasant and unwavering monotone. Giggles and whispers began. Of course I had noticed the same thing and had no doubt as to the topic and targets of the not-so-well-guarded whispers. My first thought was to save the boys from the embarrassment that would probably have led to their abandonment of the entire enterprise. In that instant, I remembered the horror stories recounted to me by adults about how their singing abilities had been ridiculed in school ("Don't sing, just mouth the words" or "You're tone deaf—you can't sing a note"). Such ridicule crippled their singing and general music-making attempts all through their childhood and into their adult lives. If I could help it, these children would not suffer the same insults. And so, I stepped in and drew attention away from the boys and their voices to the physical organization of the choir. Luckily, the boys were tall enough for me to be able to ask them to move to the back and the observant but less than sensitive young ladies could be asked to move to the front so that I would be able to easily see all of the members of the choir. Housed safely in the back row, the boys could sing their hearts out and hopefully be spared the painful anguish resulting from comments that would otherwise inevitably have been made. I must admit that this put the boys out of my immediate earshot as well. I too preferred the crystal clear voices on pitch to the half-spoken, half-sung monotones.

At this point, and for at least four months afterward, I was only concerned about sparing the feelings of the boys. I never thought about whether they would, in fact, ever learn to sing on pitch. If someone had asked me in December or January if any of them could or would ever sing accurately on pitch, I would have answered with a flat "No." I might have qualified my negative response with some statement to the effect that even though they could not sing by conventional pitch standards, they should still have the pleasure of using their voices individually or collectively for musical expression. What is important here is that I was not going to the trouble of saving them from embarrassment so that they could develop confidence and have a conducive setting in which to learn to sing. I was trying to save them from embarrassment solely for the sake of saving them from embarrassment. Admittedly, I was probably trying to save myself from the same embarrassment.

Quite frankly, I gave the matter very little thought until February. At that time we were all preparing for auditions for the musical *Mary Poppins*, which the school community produced in the spring (see Chapter 8). Children were encouraged to audition for several parts, including roles as bankers, chimney sweeps, servants, and the better known parts of Mr. and Mrs. Banks, the children Jane and Michael, and of course, Mary Poppins and Bert. The children who signed up to audition for the various parts were given a short piece of script and a verse of a song to prepare before the auditions took place.

It should come as no surprise that one of "the boys" would audition for a lead role. Sure enough, Daniel announced both to me and to the world at large that he was trying out for Bert. My immediate thought was to try to talk him out of it. As far as I was concerned, it was fine to sing in a group where his voice was only one of seventy, and well hidden at that, but it was a different situation altogether where he would be on stage in front of parents, friends, and peers, boisterously bellowing out Bert's solos.

I didn't even try to talk Daniel out of it, partly because I knew it would be to no avail, partly because I didn't want to draw attention to him, partly because I was afraid to do it, and partly because I hoped that some fortuitous circumstance would intervene and the whole situation would resolve itself.

February 10 was "Audition Day." My heart sank as Daniel,

in front of a panel of judges made up of teachers and students, very confidently and masterfully delivered his spoken lines. At least if the spoken part had been weak, I thought to myself, we might somehow have avoided the singing portion of the audition. I sat down at the piano with a heavy heart and started to play the opening to "Chim Chiminey." I winked at Daniel for luck and to cue him in. Daniel began to sing.

I was completely unprepared for his rendition of "Chim Chiminey." I expected the spark and confidence, but hearing him sing on pitch—including leaps of octave intervals—was certainly the last thing I thought I would hear. Daniel got the part.

Two things are important about that audition on February 10. For one, I almost deprived Daniel of the chance to audition because I doubted his ability. What a loss that would have been. As if a teacher has the right to determine for a child what he or she should risk or simply take part in. I would expect that if I were to have asked Daniel if he could sing "Chim Chiminey" with the right pitches, he would have been able to assess his ability, both before he mastered those pitches ("No, not yet") and after ("Yes, now I can").

The second issue here is that this child learned how to sing. How did this happen? On February 10 the part of me that thinks about documentation for research purposes wished for some sort of evidence or account detailing the change. But as I thought further about the matter, it occurred to me that doing so might have brought precisely the kind of attention to Daniel and his voice that could well have precluded the very change that occurred, namely moving from a monotonous monotone to a well-intonated performance. By not bringing attention to his voice, but by surrounding him with good singing, by giving him encouragement and guidance in making musical judgments as he improvised and composed during class time, and by providing a setting that was socially stimulating and safe, Daniel learned to sing. The relative importance of these factors cannot be measured, but all of my intuitions tell me that each of these factors was an indispensable condition that made change possible.

The story does not end with Daniel's new-found voice and success with the musical repertoire of *Mary Poppins*. Rehearsals had been ongoing for about six or seven weeks when I approached Daniel one morning with the intention of teaching him the only *Mary Poppins* song he had not yet tried. It was also one of the few Mary Poppins songs that I had not at least introduced during regular music classes. "A Man Has Dreams" has a rather complex melody with syncopation, chromatic passages, and modulations to related keys. It is also a shared song, between Bert and Mr. Banks. A rather dejected Mr. Banks tells Bert how his dreams have been shattered since "that Poppins woman" entered his household. Bert responds by appearing to sympathize with Banks, but by the end of the song, shows Banks how important it is for him to pay less attention to his troublesome career at the bank and more attention to his children before, as Bert puts it, "they've up and grown, and then they've flown, and it's too late for you to give." Daniel and I talked about the conversation in the song before I played it. Daniel was immediately taken by the message in the song and told me that he was sure to like singing this song. I was pleased at his response and thought to myself that teaching him the song should be a smooth operation of less than fifteen minutes of the morning.

As usual, I played the piano part and sang the song through for him before asking him to join in. After playing and singing it, I asked Daniel if he would like to hear it again or if he wanted to join in. I cannot recall if I played and sang it alone a second time, but it doesn't much matter one way or another. At any rate, when he was ready to sing with me, out came that unmistakable monotone. Those earlier thoughts of learning the song in fifteen minutes and having some time to myself before recess were almost instantaneously driven out by thoughts of the following sort: Where did that come from? What if the polytonal singing of the audition and earlier rehearsals was like a remission? What happens if he can't sing anything anymore? What will we do for the May performances? Do I find another Bert? Can I find another Bert? Do I want to find another Bert? What's going on here?

After we managed to plod through what had suddenly become a painfully long ditty, I gave Daniel my usual response: "Good, let's try it again." The second time through was no better, and in fact, seemed worse. Same encouraging but basically noncommittal response on my part. Third time through—same monotone, same response. Fourth time—monotone with a few fluctuations in accordance with the melodic line. Fifth time (and all times subsequently)—right on pitch. By then I was completely entranced by what I had heard and was hearing. Reflecting back, I realized then that there were two striking features of Daniel's first three attempts. Not only were they all indisputably monotonal, but the complicated dotted and syncopated rhythm structure was accurately produced from the very first time. Daniel clearly appropriated the rhythm information before the pitch information. Rhythm for Daniel was, and remains, the most salient feature in a piece of music. This is not the case for many people, including myself. I suspect that the difference can be accounted for in large part by the differences in the music of our respective cultures. Daniel listens to and performs many raps (a highly rhythmic form of music expression with percussive accompaniment and little pitch variation). I listen to and perform polyphonic music in traditional three-part harmony, where the rhythms tend to fit into predictably simple patterns of duple and triple meters. In Daniel's perception, it is the rhythm that is most important and often most interesting. In mine, it is the harmonic structure that is most important. Small wonder that he would have performed the rhythm of "A Man Has Dreams" correctly before concentrating on the pitches. However, it is also true that if Daniel had not already learned to produce those pitches in other singing contexts, it is unlikely that he would have been able to sing the song.

I have been thinking about Daniel's singing for some time, thinking not only about the factors that made his learning possible, but also on the things that commonly occur in music teaching in schools. There are two practices that I have come to regard as highly questionable.

This is the first: I believe it is wrong for music teachers to admonish children who do not sing in class. The extreme case of such admonitions is the statement "If you don't sing with everyone else, I'll make you sing a solo." I too, at the beginning, often gently chided children for not participating, and, I am sorry to admit, would even come close to singling out children who were not singing by saying, "Everyone is singing except a few sitting over there." There were two children in particular, Carol and Joanne, who would never sing. It was a source of great frustration for me, largely because I couldn't understand why they wouldn't want to sing. I finally stopped making comments about non-singers, and simply said, "If you don't want to sing, that's your choice. You can listen. The only rule is going to be that you don't talk while other people are singing." Carol, one of the two children who refused to sing for eight full months, became perhaps the strongest singer in her class during the ninth and tenth months of school. To this day, I do not know why she finally decided to sing. Maybe it was because I told her she didn't have to. Maybe it was because she finally decided that the situation was safe enough to take the risk. But whatever the reason, she always sings now—and she knows how to sing all of the songs she never sang before. Even when she was "only" listening, Carol was learning to sing.

While I was reflecting on the issues surrounding pitch production and singing, I had several conversations with other music teachers about children's ability to sing on pitch, which leads to the second practice I seriously question. It strikes me that what many music teachers do to correct pitch might in fact perpetuate the problem. Many teachers still ask children to match pitches, either singing the same note the teacher has sung or singing a note that has been played on some other instrument. When a teacher marks or grades the child on whether he or she has matched a pitch accurately, the practice is even more suspect and potentially harmful. I am sure that the chances of producing those correct pitches are markedly diminished when children know that they will be graded on their attempts. I still see these practices being perpetuated in universities and colleges purporting to train music teachers, often by former music teachers who are caught in the trap of teaching the way that they were once taught. Many times I have had undergraduate students ask about this practice and admit that they themselves "couldn't tell if a note was right, so how [am I] supposed to know if a student is singing accurately?"

The practice of marking the accuracy of isolated pitches threatens to become even more of a problem if teachers use new technology to deliver their old pedagogy. When music teachers discover that I use computers in music teaching, one of the first things some of them ask is whether there are any computer programs for pitch matching. A pitch matching program requires children to sing a pitch after it has been played by the computer, and then the computer shows the child the pitch he or she sang. The child then can check to see if the two pitches corresponded. When pitch matching as an exercise (either with or without a computer) was first brought to my attention, I felt uneasy about its use but was unable to articulate any solid reasons for my unease. Now the reasons have become obvious. If the child does not sing predictably or accurately, pitch matching exercises highlight for the child and for everybody else what the child cannot do. This type of exercise is undeniably damaging to a child's self-esteem, and might have the effect of ensuring that he or she *never* learns to sing on pitch. Also, the idea of pitch matching is, in a very fundamental way, unmusical. Pitches in isolation do not make music. Pitches only make musical sense when they are a part of a melody or harmony supporting a melody.

And pitch production, therefore, should be learned in the context of melody, not in isolation. Finally, the melodies themselves should have meaning for the child. There were good reasons for Daniel to learn to sing—social reasons as he took part in choir sessions, personal and community reasons as he learned songs for *Mary Poppins*. These reasons are very different from learning to sing because the music teacher tells or forces you to or, worse yet, because the music teacher shows you that you can't.

Singing is highly satisfying for many, many people. School singing should be the same. It should not be an exercise in perfect pitch matching or training. By all means, sing, and sing with children. But sing for the sake of singing alone.

An Evolving Knowledge of Music

·································· By the end of the school year, the children's views of music were astonishingly rich and diverse. Throughout the year they had learned a great deal about using music as a way to communicate and to interpret their worlds. I knew that they, as I, had made real and significant links between "school music" and "other music." As I stated in the first chapter, perhaps the most important change for me during the year at the Hennigan was that what I considered "school music" and "real music" began to be one and the same. So too did children perceive these boundaries to be altered. Their comments, and those of their parents, affirmed this belief. One child's father told me, "You have no idea how much you influenced Jennifer this year. Before she met you, she hated practicing the piano, and she's in Suzuki, you know, and we could never get her to read. We couldn't believe it when she asked for the sheet music for *Mary Poppins*, and began reading it, note by note."

Fourth- and fifth-grade children's comments at the end of the

1986 school year echoed, time and time again, the fact that they regarded music as something important and serious. This was evidenced in their views of themselves as composers, in their comments about what music meant to them, and in their comments about how the ways that they experienced music during the year influenced their views about music, and about other subjects as well. A small portion of these comments are reproduced below. The first set of questions deals with composition.

> Q: Do you think you learned anything about composing this year?
> A: Not really. Just about the notes.
> Q: Do you think you learned anything about how you can combine the notes?
> A: Yeah, like when were were doing the machines [Building Machines, see Chapter 6]. Everybody made a different noise and it usually sounded pretty good.
> Q: Do you think that just happened or was there some planning?
> A: Well, I think everybody before they volunteered to be a part of a machine they planned what sound they were going to make.
> Q: So you don't think just any sound would have worked?
> A: No, no, it depended on each machine.

Another child's comments on composition:

> Q: Do you think you learned anything from stuff like "Beep beep twiddle twiddle" [Body Orchestra, see Chapter 3]?
> A: Well, I don't think I learned anything, well, except how to make up sounds for different notes and rhythms. And I think it brought out my imagination because now I can think up more sounds. . . . You have to use all different kinds of sounds and different rhythms, different pitches.

A comment on making music, rather than being a passive observer:

> Q: What did you like about music this year?
> A: I just liked the things we did, you know, like we made our own instruments and used the different kinds of instruments. Instead of just watching someone else do all the work, you know what I mean? You got to do your own, you got to really try it out.

Q: What do you mean by really try it out?

A: Well, like the [Orff] bells. . . . Say you don't have a thing of bells at home, you'd never get a chance. I learned a lot about music this year. I learned, I mean, about the basic stuff, and also a lot of, well, like the notes and stuff. It's a different way of learning here. *And you learn things here that you don't learn when you're sitting with your hands folded.* [emphasis added]

And finally, the comments by a child for whom the most important thing about music was the modeling of the teacher, and how this modeling might be generalized to other disciplines:

Q: What did you think of music this year?

A: Well, the best part I liked about music is you. 'Cause you're very funny to have around, you like to joke and play music, and sing. You take it seriously, not like a joke.

Q: What should we be telling other teachers about teaching music?

A: Not only just teaching music, it's like, not only teach, but teach them so that they *want* to be taught. 'Cause that's what you do.

Q: How do you mean, teach them like they want to be taught?

A: You were like, not just a teacher, you were like putting yourself into it, like, other teachers, they'd say, "O.K., time for music class." But you would say, "Now, what do y'all want to do?" Things like, "O.K., you know what I think?" Like showing your feelings and everything.

Q: Do you think that's important for other subjects besides music, or just music?

A: Yeah. A lot of subjects. *Every* subject.

Although many will recognize the significance of comments like these, it is true that these observations were made by the children during the final glow of a successful year. It is therefore much more important that now, several years later, some of the children that I occasionally meet by chance or design are *still* influenced by their music experiences at the Hennigan. Some have continued to compose outside of school, sometimes sharing these later compositions with me. Some have taken up private music study. Many still comment on the type of "teaching" that they had in music, often comparing it to "regular school."

I am sure that one reason that these results occurred is that children valued what we were doing and knew that I valued my involvement with them. As Whitehead (1929) so aptly put it, we must not engage children in mere "intellectual minuets." That children are accustomed to doing things that have no meaning for them was never more clearly stated to me than by a young girl who had spent an entire school day at the Hennigan either working with Lego/LOGO or building props for the *Mary Poppins* production. She stated, "This was the greatest day. I didn't do any work at all, just Lego and props. I didn't even pick up a pencil *unless I needed one*" [emphasis added].

Of course, she had in fact worked very hard during the day, and the day passed very quickly (she also commented that "It always seems like we get here and it's already time to go"). What she meant by not having done any work at all was that she hadn't done any teacher assigned "school work." A colleague of mine once related the following observation by a ten-year-old lad: "Work is what the teacher tells us to do. Play is what we want to do. If the teacher tells us how to play, then that's work."

The music playground would not have been sustained without the kinds of relationships that I have described between myself and the students, and those that grew between myself and other teachers. What I have described would also not have been possible had there not been learning on the part of *both* students and teachers, had there not been numerous open-ended materials and tools, had there not been a rich variety of musical experiences, had there not been flexibility in the teaching, had there not been structures in the environment, and had there not been ownership of the learning, the activities, and the environment on the part of teachers and children. I would like to explore further this notion of "learning" and, more specifically, how one goes about evaluating such learning.

In the second chapter, when I first described a music playground, I related many of the features of the playground—structure, materials, tools, my roles as playground monitor, activity leader, and learner—and I claimed that a great deal of learning took place as a result. Peppered throughout the preceding pages is evidence of the kind of learning I was thinking of. However, having made the assertion that one can learn through play, it is natural to ask how I know that people are learning in the playground or, perhaps, precisely what it is that people learn. What each person learns, child and adult alike, is as individual as each person. But my conviction that children are learning comes *not* from testing them after they have played. It comes from the kinds of spontaneous comments and observations as those just related. Evidence of learning also comes from watching them solve the problems that they naturally encounter in such an environment. When a child is composing a melody on the keyboard, he or she learns or creates a notation to remember the melody as the need arises. When a child is building a motorized car using Lego/LOGO and the car moves too quickly, the child learns how to use gears to slow the car down. When a child is planning a puppet show, he or she writes down the story line as it develops. Learning is apparent in the products that the children create, as well as in the development of those products.

One of the usual responses to the claim that learning is occurring is that there should be some way to measure that learning. In school, this is usually done by assigning children a mark based on some measurement of their understanding of some subject. In a music playground, the children are never marked on their work. There are no requirements to fulfill, no hoops to jump through, no uniform standards to achieve. One child's composition is never judged against another's. It would seem absurd to mark children on recess. It seems equally absurd to me to mark children on their arts constructions. How would I mark a game of marbles? How would I assign a grade to a child's composition? Or, for that matter, how would I give Beethoven a grade on his Seventh Symphony? Why would I want to? It was clear that if I were to assign marks, they would be a trivial reflection of the playing and learning involved in the creation of the children's works. Assigning marks would also invariably have led to situations where all children would have had to jump through the same hoop ("Let's all write a round today"), whether or not they wanted to or were ready to do so. For, the argument goes, how else can one standardize or be objective? How else could marks have meaning? It is my belief that marks almost never have meaning, no matter how "objective." At best, they confirm what the student already judged about his or her performance. At worst, they leave children with the impression that they are dumb or stupid in comparison with their peers.

However, to say that children were never graded in a summative fashion is not to say that there was no formative or functional evaluation of their work. On the contrary, there was constant evaluation, observation, examination, judgment, reflection, change, reevaluation, and so on. But such evaluation is undeniably different from the process of "giving grades." For one, the evaluations were constructively offered to make the piece better portray the mood and message intended by the child. Thus, they were of the form "I like the way you used the minor third. Maybe you could use it again later if you want to make this part sound sad as well." They were not of the form "That F sharp is wrong. There is no F sharp in B flat minor." This kind of evaluation and revision was ongoing, and made easier by the fact that I kept all of the children's compositions available in folders on open shelves where they could have access to them as readily as I. (Every child had his or her own storage space.) Sometimes we would go back to "old favorites" a few months later, and a child might play it again, or add to it, or change the notation form. Occasionally, I asked a child to work a little more on a piece, or I might help him or her with harmony, especially if the piece had promise and with a little "expert" editing might be even more pleasing. However, when I did this, I was careful not to add too much. On a few occasions, having made that mistake, children were left feeling that the piece was no longer "theirs."

It should come as no surprise that I, the "teacher," was not the only evaluator in the classroom. In fact, often when I offered advice, perhaps about harmony or instrumentation, children firmly and gently informed me, "I like the way it goes. I'm not changing that part." They similarly listened to, considered, and rejected or accepted, in whole or in part, the suggestions of their peers. But regardless of the outcome of the freely offered advice, all of us accorded strong respect to each other's work and criticisms, out of mutual respect for each other's membership in our learning community, our playground.

A few years after my year at the Hennigan, one of my former students overheard a conversation I was having with one of my undergraduate students regarding the "giving of grades" and commented, "She doesn't give grades. It's a lot better that way 'cause you learn more."

I am sure that all of us learned more by not having to get caught up in the giving and receiving of grades (one of the luxuries often associated with teaching an arts subject—but need this luxury be limited to the arts?). We have, for one thing, more time to learn because our time isn't taken up with writing and marking assignments for the purpose of grading. While the children had folders of their compositions, which they would revise from time to time, identifying their favorites as they went along, these were collections of pieces, not for the purpose of grading but for the purpose of collecting pieces that they had written. This is somewhat like the use of writing folders as employed by those ascribing to a process writing approach (see Atwell 1987, Graves 1983, Murray 1985).

It is a combination of all of the things I have summarized in the chapter thus far that made it possible for the making of music to evolve in the ways that it did, and to continue to evolve in the ways I have described. I would like to make one final observation.

I have come to believe that the person or people who benefit most from the development of a music teaching approach are those who do the developing. I would argue that this is just the same as someone who learns a great deal by programming a computer math drill, but with the result that the students who eventually use the program learn little. This might mean that I will ultimately learn more than those who read this book, because my own music teaching and personal music development have been radically altered by my experiences with children. But I hope that what I have described is flexible enough for others to shape, making it fit their own musical development and teaching settings. What I have described is certainly malleable enough for me to continue to grow musically and to find new ways to inspire children to make meaning through music. For music, as any other discipline, should be a dynamic, evolving knowledge. And that evolving knowledge should come from active participation in the discipline, participation that is shared, participation that is enjoyed. Above all, it is critical that we never ask children to do things that we wouldn't willingly do ourselves. How many of us ever buy a gift for someone else that we wouldn't like to keep? We need to give children the *musical* gifts that we would, and do, give ourselves.

Teachers as Mentors:
Betty Ferguson

·································· IN some ways, this chapter may
seem like something of a departure from the earlier chapters. It is.
It is about a woman who helped me become a musician in the
broadest sense and showed me how to find the courage, within
myself and from my students, to become a teacher. It seemed a
fitting conclusion to a book that is meant to convey a love for
learning about music and, indeed, a love for learning.

In the first chapter, I said that my aim was not to produce a
method for teaching music, but to offer possibilities that might be
adapted to a particular context—a context that includes the inter-
dependence of teacher, students, community, and culture. Every
once in a while, we need to remind ourselves that it is not the
teaching methods or approaches themselves that make the difference. The teacher is much more important than the method. Many
a fine teacher has taught by the most traditional methods. Likewise,
even the ideas contained in the preceding chapters can be used
with poor results (recall the teacher described in Chapter 9 who

cut straws for her children). Ultimately, the continual evolution of a teaching approach rests in the hands of the teacher and his or her interaction with the children. Different approaches and ideas are constantly being proposed by educational researchers and curriculum developers. Some may be retained by particular teachers, some may not. The one constant factor is the teacher.

Most of us remember one or two outstanding teachers especially well, teachers who in some sense became mentors—people who not only taught but guided, counseled, inspired, and took a personal interest in our overall development. Some of our memories of those teachers, no doubt, became somewhat romanticized over time, but we can often recall incidents with amazing clarity, probably because they were in some sense pivotal to our thinking and formative growth.

Numerous people have tried to ascertain just what it is that makes someone a "good teacher." Studies that describe people's views of teachers years later (e.g., Kuehnle 1984) indicate that while people often have strong memories about the teacher that influenced them most, the descriptions of those teachers are remarkable for their diversity. Some favorite teachers and mentors are remembered as stern and exacting. Others are remembered as humorous and entertaining. Often, these teachers are remembered for their love and understanding of their discipline and for the way that they made the subject interesting to those who were studying it. In any case, since it appears difficult if not impossible to describe these special teachers as a homogeneous group of people, researchers often resort to describing particular individuals in trying to convey those characteristics that mark a teacher as special, at least for some of his or her students.

It is in this spirit that I introduce Mrs. Ferguson. Betty Ferguson was my piano teacher and my mentor. She died from cancer as I was thinking about writing this book. At that time there was no Chapter 12 on Mrs. Ferguson, but there is no more fitting way to end *This Too is Music*. In fact, this *is* music.

My family moved to Calgary, Alberta, from a small town in British Columbia when I was thirteen years old. One of the hardships of moving was giving up a piano teacher of whom I was very fond and facing the difficult task of finding another. I called the local conservatory and was given a list of names. Over the next few days I contacted several teachers, including Mrs. Ferguson. I liked the sound of her voice. Although she told me she had already taken on more pupils than she could handle (something I'm sure she said every September for over sixty years), she agreed to listen to me play, and an audition was arranged.

It was a cool and windy September day when I first met Mrs. Ferguson. I was scheduled to audition for lessons at two o'clock in the afternoon. On other occasions, an audition went something like this: arrive at the appointed time, play excerpts from a select repertoire, make a quiet exit twenty minutes later. Not this time. Mrs. Ferguson spent the first twenty minutes—what I expected to be the length of the entire audition—talking to me. We talked about school, my recent move to Calgary, the fall weather, and a hike she was planning to take in a few weeks. She then asked me whether I thought the wind blowing through the trees made music in a major or a minor key. That may well have been the first time I found myself speechless. "Sweet old lady," I thought to myself. "That must be what happens to you when you get old." I cannot remember what my answer to her was then, but I know that now I could speak at length about music in the trees—and on the beach, in the swamp, in the kitchen, and on a subway train, besides. Her question about the wind and the trees was to be the first of many ways that she was to show me how music was, as she put it, "something inside me." Mrs. Ferguson was my first and my best model of how to *live* music.

The "sweet old lady," of course, was anything but the slightly senile woman I first imagined her to be. In fact, when I finally did play for her, I thought I could impress her with my very fast and very loud performance of the "Valse Romantique" by Claude Debussy. Not so. She didn't even want to hear it. Instead, she asked me to play a Bach three-part Invention, without a doubt the most difficult piece on the list I had given her, and certainly the piece that I was least prepared to play. Somehow, by her very choice, I realized that she was aware of this too. My only hope was that she would stop me partway through. And so, I sat at her Heintzman grand piano, listened to the wind in the trees, somehow convinced myself not to attack the piece at a breakneck speed, and played. The performance (of the whole piece) was not as bad as it might have been, but it was far from brilliant. Her comment was brief and piercing: "Well dear, you have a good ear. You *could* learn to play Bach well."

I did learn to play Bach well, and a whole lot of other things too. Mrs. Ferguson was a superb teacher, a patient craftsman, a skilled technician, a fine musician, and in time, a valued colleague and friend. But what was most important was that I learned that music was not something that you did during 6:30–8:30 A.M. practice and Wednesday evening lessons, but something that you lived and breathed. It was because of this I learned to play. As is the case with many young pianists, I had poor technique and hated practicing scales. No wonder, since to me scales were not music—they were a necessary evil designed by music teachers and conservatory examiners, which, like cod liver oil and Oxford shoes, were supposed to be "good for you." But to Mrs. Ferguson scales were music. "Listen to A major," she said to me, "it's the brightest of all of the major scales, don't you think?" By this time, having begun to appreciate the music in the trees, hearing and making music out of scales became possible, and later inevitable.

Predictably during those teenage years, the kind of self-discipline demanded by Mrs. Ferguson and by the music itself was something I wasn't always able to sustain. One of the times I let my devilish streak surface in her presence was at a "playing class." Playing classes were rather informal monthly gatherings of as many of her pupils and their friends and parents who could come. Music was played and discussed, parents or other siblings often joined in the music making on instruments of their own, and there were always cakes and cookies to make the afternoon even more pleasant. It was in such a setting that I charged through a Chopin waltz with much more speed and volume than either she or Chopin would ever have approved of. The audience responded as I knew they would—they were impressed with the "show" and applauded at length. What could Mrs. Ferguson say? As usual, a few words (delivered with a smile) that were impossible to forget: "Well dear, that was brilliantly inaccurate!"

Besides the rather informal performance setting of the playing class, Mrs. Ferguson encouraged all of her pupils to play in recitals, concerts, and festivals. I loved to perform, and participated in these settings frequently. Of course, there were times when I became very nervous before playing. Mrs. Ferguson once told me that nervousness implied that I had respect for the audience, and over the years I've noticed that the times when I'm most nervous are indeed those times when I value the people in the audience for their musical sensitivity and intelligence. However, as she well knew, respecting one's audience does nothing to minimize the butterflies in the stomach. In fact, reminding yourself of how much you respect your audience usually has the opposite effect. I remember one occasion particularly well. I was competing in a music festival in an open class for Bach Preludes and Fugues. This meant that anyone could enter the competition, playing one of the forty-eight Preludes and Fugues that Bach had composed. I was one of some twenty competitors, and much younger than most. Also, I recognized two or three pianists as perhaps the best young musicians in the city, and the idea of even playing in the same arena knowing that they would be listening terrified me, never mind the fact that I was competing against them. We were all sitting roughly in the order of the program. I was eighth on the list. Mrs. Ferguson was sitting right beside me and I'm sure could sense that this time I was more concerned than usual. It was a situation that I desperately wanted to get out of—I even considered suddenly becoming sick and fleeing for the door! She whispered to me that ninety-nine years from now, what happened that evening would not matter one bit, and in fact, "even next week you'll have more important things in your life to think about." Most important, though, she told me to love the music and listen as I played. My performance of the Bach was probably the best public performance I have ever given. I have played well since, but never did I enjoy playing a piece so much in public and never was I less aware of the fact that there was an audience in the room. Love the music, and listen.

There were times, too, that I played badly and shouldn't have. Often it was because I was less prepared than I might have been, or simply because my mind was elsewhere. Those were the times when I complained most loudly about the piano—the action was too heavy, the action was too light, the tone was too thin, the tone was too rich. Just once (I didn't need any other reminders), after registering such a complaint, Mrs. Ferguson quietly chastised me, "It's not the horse, dear, it's the rider." How true, although I have over the years sometimes rightfully complained about a piano, for it is also true that better horses make a difference to the rider. But first the rider has to know how to coax the horse to trot, canter, and gallop.

It was around this time, in my mid-teens, that I began giving piano lessons myself. Only then did I realize that Mrs. Ferguson too had something at stake when her students performed, even though she never let her own fears and doubts show. But one of her strengths was the unshakable faith she had in her students—and we all knew that, no matter which horse we found ourselves riding, she would never let us fall, or at least not with serious injury. And her faith was not misplaced—in time we developed enough faith in ourselves to play and learn as we judged best.

It was also during those teenage years that Mrs. Ferguson became a confidante—someone to talk to about boyfriend problems, parent problems, and all of the other universal problems of growing up. There were many lessons when I hardly played at all, for she knew that there are times when playing the piano helps, and times when it doesn't. But by no means did she merely sympathize and encourage me to maintain a state of self-pity. I remember one evening in particular where I was sure she would feel sorry for me and my lot. After I told my tale of woe she asked me, "What was the best thing that happened to you today?" Struck speechless again. Before I had a chance to answer she added, "It should never take you that long to figure it out. Something good happens to everyone, every day. Even if it's only a little thing, like having the bus driver smile at you and ask you how you are. Think of those things when you go to sleep at night."

When I announced to the world at large that I planned to be a teacher, the reactions were mixed. Some were disappointed, but quiet. My father was disappointed and vocal: "You are not going to be *just* a teacher. Don't waste your brains on that!" A few were mildly encouraging. Mrs. Ferguson, from whom I expected unqualified enthusiasm, said, "I see. Well dear, if you are brave enough to teach, you must never stop learning." She had an uncanny ability to say the very thing that would throw me off my feet. This notion of *teacher as learner* was something that I saw in action every time we met, and it was to become second nature to me as I became a teacher myself.

Our relationship first began to change when I was accepted into a summer program at the Banff School of Fine Arts in Banff, Alberta. She had encouraged me to apply, helped me prepare an audition tape, and given me many pointers when I was granted a live audition (of the typical twenty-minute nature that I had once expected from her). When I left for the summer, she told me that my new teacher would likely offer different advice on points of interpretation and technique than she and for me to heed his suggestions even if I knew them to be different from hers. At the time, I was six months away from my final music examination, which was to lead to my becoming an Associate of the Royal Conservatory of Music of the University of Toronto. Her feeling was that I would benefit more from my intense study with a new teacher were I to give myself wholly to him, listening to his teaching, responding to his suggestions, than by remaining loyal to her. Although she had always encouraged me to make my own interpretations of repertoire, I realized then that it was within the framework she had established. On the eve of my departure to Banff (and beyond), she made it clear that there was more than one such framework and that my own musical choices would be deeper if I was able to understand the framework of another. My teacher at Banff was someone she respected highly: it was an example of how two well-informed views could sometimes conflict, but nevertheless both reflect musically intelligent choices. Her advice was sealed with the endorsement that when I returned for my final exam, she would act as a coach rather than teacher, helping me perfect the repertoire on the basis of the summer experience.

Mrs. Ferguson was true to her word, and as coach taught me just as much as before. Looking back, I realize her support of the Banff experience was one way of showing me that I was ready to begin making my own musical decisions and that such decisions should be made without pre-judgment, based on an open-minded examination of several viable alternatives. It was also a way of showing me that the choices were, in fact, mine to make and that the most a teacher, or coach, could do was to present alternatives. I also knew, even at that time, that it was her way of saying that it was time for me to grow on my own—in a formal teaching situation, she had given me all that she had to give. She drove me to the examination center one cold January morning. Before I went in, she gave me a very old brooch, wrapped in Kleenex (things like gift wrapping and cooking were not her strong points). Her mother had given her the brooch on the day that she played her final exam at the London Royal School of Music. Mrs. Ferguson told me that I would likely be her last A.R.C.T. student since she was retiring that spring (she came out of retirement two years later and taught for another ten years) and that, on such a special day, she wanted me to have something to remember her by, at the same time apologizing that the brooch wasn't real gold but inexpensive costume jewelry from the 1920s. I was deeply moved and hesitated to tell her that I did not want her to stay during the exam, for fear she would think that I wasn't grateful or didn't need her anymore. As I was groping for words, she briskly announced that she was on her way, told me to play well, and call her when the exam was over. I did play well, and as I was walking out, I wished that she had been there after all. As I turned the corner, she stood up from her chair. She grinned, and I knew immediately that she had been there the entire time. For she knew not only that her presence would have unnerved me going in, but that when it was over, I would have wished her to be there.

Eight months later, at seventeen, I packed a trunk and left for a university two thousand miles away from Calgary. I was enrolled as an arts student in psychology and mathematics. For almost a year, I only once played the piano. That one time was disastrous: fifteen minutes was enough to convince me that I had forgotten everything I once knew and that I would never play again. When I returned to Calgary in the spring, I was afraid that when I visited Mrs. Ferguson she would ask me to play and my lapse would be exposed. She didn't. We spent the entire time discussing my new university life, and when I left I thought I had finally pulled the wool over her eyes. The next spring I returned to Calgary again, brimming with news about a 'cellist with whom I was playing chamber music on a regular basis. "So you've found music again," she commented. Every time after that she always asked me to play, once even asking me "what I had *prepared.*"

Our relationship underwent yet another change only a couple of years before she died. The last time I saw her, and subsequent times when we wrote and talked to each other on the phone, we were no longer teacher and pupil or coach and performer, but colleagues in the learning business. That day she asked me how I dealt with certain technical problems, and we engaged in a long discussion and together experimented with our various techniques. I then shared with her some of my own compositions, timidly and anonymously. Her interest was genuine, and she used two or three of my compositions for children with her own students. I cherish many of her words, and perhaps most of all these: "Well dear, I think you must be a very fine teacher. Your students are lucky to have you. It is so important, this new work you do with composition and computers. I wish I was one of your kids."

We played solos and duets for many hours, and as the afternoon became the evening, we stopped for dinner and contemplated how we would spend the next few hours before I had to leave to catch a midnight "red-eye-special" flight for Toronto. She had that playful glint in her eye. What next? I thought to myself, thinking that all I really wanted to do was sleep. But no—Mrs. Ferguson had a movie that she wanted to watch on the VCR, and as we laughed over Superman II (she'd already seen Superman I), I thought about how much fun it would be to see what she would be like as she grew old. For she was a young woman of seventy-five. As she wrapped her svelte dancer's body in a black fur coat and drove me to the airport a few hours later, I marveled at her beauty—she still had masses of red hair, now streaked with white, rosy cheeks, laughing eyes, and boundless love, energy, and wisdom. In my eyes nothing could defeat her.

When I heard of her death, my first thought was to cancel my classes and spend the day at home in tears. I imagined almost immediately what her reaction would likely have been: "Now dear, it's alright to be sad, but you mustn't disappoint your students. You'll be playing and laughing again before the day is out." And I was. The "best thing" that happened that day was a young child's comment during his lesson as we were improvising in the blues style: "That's not playing the piano. That's playing music. I love music, don't you?" I do love music, and I loved Mrs. Ferguson and I miss her. She gave me much, much more than the brooch to remember her by.

This too is music.

Afterword

·· I HAVE stated more than once here that I am not attempting to describe a sequential or developmental method for teaching music. I am sure that if someone took the activities described in this book as an exact blueprint for teaching elementary music, he or she would find that the same techniques and ideas *would not work* the same way in a different setting. Too many variables would change. The teacher would be different, the children, possibly the culture, the resources, and so on. What is important here, more than the activities and techniques, is the type of learning environment features that were outlined and described in the first chapter. If these features constitute a method, then at least the method is a highly variable one, depending on the people involved. Perhaps it is better called an "approach," a term adopted by those practicing Kodaly and Orff techniques. For the things that I do change with each new group of people I encounter. I am never quite sure what the outcome of a workshop with teachers, an undergraduate class, a guest appearance in a regular classroom, or a private piano lesson will be. This is not to say that I have no goals or standards. I want people to enjoy what they are doing and to léarn something about music in the process. But I cannot, nor do I want to, begin to predict or set conditions so that a certain kind of learning takes place for everyone involved. Not only does such a position assume some sort of static state regarding musical knowledge, but it assumes that I can predict what someone else will learn. This is simply not the case.

Some music teachers, however, adhere to a music teaching method or approach, and with considerable success. I would be remiss if I were to omit a discussion of the well-known music teaching methods and approaches that currently figure prominently in many North American and European school systems and in private music teaching. Amongst such methods are the Kodaly and Orff approaches, Dalcroze Eurhythmics, and the Suzuki Method. All of these have value. All are driven by firmly held beliefs stemming out of years of practice, both by those responsible for instigating the methods and approaches and by those who have steadfastly seen to their implementation. However, if any approach becomes more important than the outcome, that is, if teachers are more concerned about "following the method" than listening to the voices of their students, then even though the performance results might be commendable, I would argue that something about music as a part of life may be sacrificed for those performance results.

Sometimes teachers are criticized for adopting and adapting parts of different approaches in what is perceived as a piecemeal fashion. I suppose that I am guilty of this practice, having used Orff instruments and approaches, Dalcroze exercises, Suzuki repertoire, and Kodaly songs. But I suspect that other teachers who do this, as I, do so because they see the value in whatever parts they adopt *for the children they are working with at a given time*. This adaptation of ideas, techniques, and activities is something that I encourage, especially when beginning teachers wonder if it is acceptable to take from one method and another.

Not only is it acceptable, in my view, to borrow from different music teaching approaches, but it is also a good thing for a teacher to take *any* exploratory activity that he or she is comfortable with and use it as a springboard for teaching music. For example, one primary teacher, who felt that her strongest teaching was in the area of science, began using music in her classroom by having children experiment with glass bottles filled with water (see Chapter 9). She felt comfortable having children manipulate the "scientific variables" (e.g., the size of the jar and the amount of water), realizing that they were beginning to also experiment with the musical effects. The children began bringing other "sound makers" from home, again experimenting with the qualities and varieties of sounds that could be produced, using the teacher's ideas with their new materials. As the year progressed, the students began making up compositions for their instruments and developing notations to record their pieces (see Chapter 7). Thus, the teacher had effectively created a classroom environment where music could be explored, using her interest in the physical sciences to extend whatever musical background she possessed (Borstad 1989). I am sure that this is only one of many possible ways that teachers without formal training in music can make music in their classrooms, using the rich experiences they have in related domains. Any teacher can set conditions for making sounds, listening to sounds, experimenting with sounds and enjoying the sounds that he or she and the children make, later recording those sounds and developing ways of sharing them with others.

Appendix:
Some Music
Playground
Resources

ONE could write hundreds of pages describing classroom materials for teaching music. What I offer here is not intended as a comprehensive list, but as an indication of the kinds of resources that teachers might use to equip a music playground. I have limited the descriptions to three categories: (1) Orff instruments, (2) synthesizers, and (3) computer software. Of the three, the Orff instruments are least likely to change over time, and predictably, the computer resources are going to change faster than one can keep up with them. Thus, I have tried to describe in a generic way the features of computer programs that are well suited to improvisation and composition, delineating criteria that might be applied to new software that is developed.

In any case, it is important to remember that there are hundreds of resources already available in most schools: art materials, miscellaneous rhythm instruments, tape recorders, perhaps a piano, and of course, the "natural" resources that we all bring to music settings—our voices and our ability to listen and move to music.

Orff Instruments

The Orff instruments include several "families" of pitched instruments, representing a variety of timbres (quality of sound). Although the original Orff complement included such instruments as viols and lutes, most of the pitched instruments found in schools today are a form of percussion instrument, commonly referred to as "xylophones." In addition, there are tuned timpani (drums) and a number of rhythm instruments. Some of the more common Orff instruments are listed below:

- Xylophones (made from wood)—Bass, Alto, Soprano.
- Metallophones (made from metal)—Bass, Alto, Soprano.
- Glockenspiels (made from a lighter metal)—Alto, Soprano, Sopranino.
- Rhythm Instruments—triangles, tambourines, hand drums, cymbals, bells, wood blocks, and so on.

A complete set of Orff instruments is *very* expensive and, therefore, it is really not feasible for each classroom to have a full complement. (A set of xylophones, metallophones, and glockenspiels, without the bass instruments, at the time of printing, were about $1000–$1800 U.S.; with the two bass instruments, about $3500 U.S.) Even though it would be great to have a full set, one should also bear in mind that during my year at the Hennigan, we had only two metallophones permanently housed in the music playground (about $450 U.S.). Most schools have some Orff instruments, or instruments like them, which are usually shared amongst teachers and children. Orff instruments are generally of exceptionally high quality and last a long time—even in schools! They are well worth the investment, although instruments made by children are also important and add a greater variety of sound (see Chapter 9). When purchasing Orff instruments, you should bear in mind that there are many different manufacturers and, consequently, some variation in quality and style.

Synthesizers

Investing in an electronic synthesizer keyboard is also money well spent. Many music stores carry them, and they can be purchased from department stores as well. Most synthesizers are made to last, and the variety of sounds that can be produced on them is staggering. They can be bought for very little money—around $45 U.S.—but I would recommend spending a little more (up to $350 U.S.) for the following features:

- Full-sized keys, four octaves or more.
- Possibility to record one or more voices directly on the keyboard.
- A large variety of preset timbres, especially unusual sounds like "guagh," "vibes," "musicbox," "ice blocks," "bubbles," "log drum," etc.
- Jacks to allow use of external microphone(s), amplifier, headphones, and audiotape recording.

If your budget can handle the strain of a couple of hundred extra dollars (in 1990, about $500 U.S. and more), a MIDI (Musical Instrument Digital Interface) synthesizer can be purchased. A MIDI equipped synthesizer, along with a MIDI processing unit (a little box), can be used to communicate with a computer. This means that music can be played on the synthesizer, "understood" by the computer, and a number of functions using a computer program can then be used. For example, many computer programs will allow the user to "edit" their compositions and to print a musical score, much like a word processing program is used to edit and print text. With some programs, segments can be manipulated (e.g., retrograde, inversion, transposition, etc.). However, it is not necessary to have a MIDI equipped synthesizer to use a computer music program. During the year at the Hennigan, in fact, the synthesizer we used was not MIDI equipped. But that was 1985—eons ago in "technology time"!

Computer Software

General Features for Consideration

Music software programs that are "open-ended" in nature are the most appealing for creative uses with children. By open-ended programs I mean those that can be used for a number of purposes, and by people of varying degrees of skill. One type of program falling under this category is the music editor, which, like a word processor, allows people to make up music, edit it, play it, and print it. In contrast, programs that I view as less useful, within the context of the approach presented in this book, are those that drill, teach, and/or test specific music concepts, such as note naming or chord identification programs.

Of the various music editors or music composition programs available for personal computers commonly found in schools, a number of features make them easier and more satisfying to use. These features include, but are certainly not limited to, the following:

- Ease of entering musical material, either with an input device, such as a mouse, joystick, or koala pad, or directly by an electronic keyboard connected to the computer by a MIDI.
- Ease of manipulation of segments of music.
- Variety of manipulations that can be made once music is entered (e.g., cut and paste, copy, insert, transpose, change tempo, key, time signature, retrograde, inversion, augmentation, diminution, etc.).
- Type of notation used by the program—it need not necessarily be standard notation, but is the notation one that children and teachers can readily understand?
- Ease of printing of scores.
- Quality of sound, both with and without MIDI.

Specific Programs

I would be surprised if anyone ever managed to create a comprehensive up-to-date list of computer music software. The list of programs described herein is anything *but* extensive, and in fact, I have listed very few programs by name. There are literally hundreds and thousands of possibilities, and the choice of music programs will depend on availability of software, cost of software (a great deal of music software falls in the $20 to $100 U.S. range), type of personal computers used, and technical support within your geographic area. Thus, I have limited the discussion of specific programs to those that I have mentioned in the text (i.e., Musicland, Melody Manipulations, and Lego/LOGO) and examples of other types that I have used or seen in use in classrooms in the past few years.

Musicland and Melody Manipulations *(for the ICON, available from the Ministry of Education, Ontario, Canada)*

These are two of the earliest music composition programs created for use by child and adult composers. They were used extensively during the 1985–86 school year at the Hennigan on the Apple IIe. Unfortunately, they are no longer available for the Apple IIe, but they are now available for the ICON. Both allow the user to enter music using a koala pad (Apple IIe) or track ball (ICON), make a variety of manipulations of the music, play it, and so on. Musicland uses a non-standard notation for rhythm (bars representing the duration of the note) and standard notation for pitch. Melody Manipulations is entirely in standard notation and is limited to the D minor pentatonic scale. Musicland and Melody Manipulations are used without MIDI with the Apple IIe and with MIDI with the ICON.

Instant Music *(for the Commodore 64, Commodore 128, Amiga, Apple II GS)*

Instant Music is a simple program to use and offers some interesting possibilities for early computer investigations. It runs without a MIDI and comes with a library of prerecorded songs. Entry is by mouse or a similar input device, and like Musicland, a gesture can be made on the input device to represent a musical line. Notation is non-standard; for example, color is used in an interesting manner. There is also a "jam along" feature, where prerecorded accompaniments can be played along with one's tune. At present, music cannot be printed from Instant Music.

Concertware *(for the Macintosh Plus, with or without MIDI)*

This is an excellent and quite sophisticated music composition program for the Macintosh. Nevertheless, it can be used by young composers, as well as by adult composers. Nearly all of the features listed previously are present in Concertware. Entry is either with a mouse or through a MIDI synthesizer, sound quality through the MIDI is excellent and quite palatable through the computer itself, a large variety of manipulations can be made (with the exception of retrograde and inversion), and printed scores are both beautiful and easy to produce. Standard notation is used to write music, and a notation similar to that of Musicland is used for the playback mode.

There are many superb music composition programs for the Macintosh. If you have a Macintosh computer at your disposal, it would be best to examine a number of them before making your final choice(s!).

Lego/LOGO *(for the Apple IIe, IBM PC)*
This is a brilliant combination of the construction set Lego with the LOGO computing language. Something built from Lego, including the familiar red, blue, and yellow bricks as well as the less familiar gears, pulleys, sensors, etc. can be controlled through a LOGO program. For example, a child might build a car that runs for a specified period of time, turning when it encounters obstacles (such as walls). Children have also built and controlled sewing machines, boats, washing machines, merry-go-rounds, walking robots, and so on. While this program is not obviously linked with music, the possibilities of construction are endless, and people can build artifacts specific to their domains. For example, using Lego and some metal pipes, I once built a "reversible tune player"—a machine that could play two melodies, depending on which direction the mallet moved across the pipes.

Lego/LOGO comes as a kit with LogoWriter (the computer program), Lego pieces, an interface box, and a whole host of curriculum ideas for teachers. It is available both in the United States and Canada for about $500 U.S.

Music Construction Set *(for the IBM Tandy, Commodore 64, Commodore 128, Atari, Atari ST, Apple II, II+, IIe, II GS)*
Deluxe Music Construction Set *(for the Macintosh, Amiga, IBM PC)*
The Music Construction Set and Deluxe Music Construction Set (with MIDI) are similar to the Concertware program for the Macintosh, described previously. The Music Construction Set is somewhat simpler in scope, but nevertheless offers many of the features identified earlier. One of these software programs is probably available for almost any personal computer found in schools throughout North America and Europe.

References and Bibliography of Influential Works

ASHTON-WARNER, S. 1963. *Teacher*. New York: Simon and Schuster.

ATWELL, N. 1987. *In the Middle: Writing, Reading, and Learning with Adolescents*. Portsmouth, N.H.: Boynton/Cook.

BORSTAD, J. 1989. *But I've Been Pouring Sounds All Day*. Presented at the annual meeting of the Canadian Society for the Study of Education (CSSE), Quebec City, Quebec, Canada.

COCHRANE, J. 1981. *The One-Room School in Canada*. Markham, Ontario: Fitzhenry & Whiteside Ltd.

DAVIES, P. M. 1967. *The Arts and Current Tendencies in Education*. London: George C. Harrap & Co. Ltd.

DENNISON, G. 1969. *The Lives of Children: The Story of the First Street School*. New York: Random House.

DE SAINT EXUPERY, A. 1943. *The Little Prince*. New York: Harcourt, Brace, & World.

DEWEY, J. 1900. *The School and Society*. Chicago: The University of Chicago Press.

DONALDSON, M. 1980. *Children's Minds*. Glasgow: Fontana/William Collins and Sons.

FALBEL, A. 1989. *Friskolen 70: An Ethnographically Informed Inquiry into the Social Context of Learning*. Unpublished doctoral thesis, Learning and Epistemology Group, Media Lab, Massachusetts Institute of Technology, Cambridge, Massachusetts.

GARDNER, H. 1983. *Frames of Mind: The Theory of Multiple Intelligences*. New York: Basic Books.

GIBRAN, K. 1986. *The Prophet*. New York: Alfred Knopf.

GILLIGAN, C. 1982. *In a Different Voice*. Cambridge, Mass.: Harvard University Press.

GIONO, J. 1989. *The Man Who Planted Trees*. London: Peter Owen.

GRAVES, D. 1983. *Writing: Teachers and Children at Work*. Portsmouth, N.H.: Heinemann.

HAWKINS, D. 1974. *The Informed Vision*. New York: Agathon Press.

HERNDON, J. 1971. *How to Survive in Your Native Land*. New York: Simon and Schuster.

HOLT, J. 1967, 1983. *How Children Learn*. New York: Dell.

KUEHNLE, A. 1984. *Teachers Remembered*. Unpublished Master of Arts paper, University of Chicago.

KOENING, B. 1973. "Messing about in Music." In C. Silberman, ed., *The Open Classroom Reader*. New York: Random House.

McLAREN, P. 1980. *Cries from the Corridor*. New York: Methuen.

MILLER, H. 1952. *The Books in My Life*. London: Peter Owen.

MURRAY, D. 1985. *A Writer Teaches Writing*. 2nd ed. Boston, Mass.: Houghton Mifflin.

PAPERT, S. 1980. *Mindstorms: Children, Computers, and Powerful Ideas*. New York: Basic Books.

POLANYI, M. 1958, 1964. *Personal Knowledge: Towards a Post-Critical Philosophy*. Chicago: University of Chicago Press.

SCHAFER, R. M. 1975. *The Rhinoceros in the Classroom*. Toronto: Universal Edition.

SCHÖN, D. A. 1983. *The Reflective Practitioner: How Professionals Think in Action*. New York: Basic Books.

SCHWEBEL, M., and RALPH, J., eds. 1973. *Piaget in the Classroom*. New York: Basic Books.

SELDEN, G. 1960. *The Cricket in Times Square*. New York: Dell.

SILBERMAN, C., ed. 1973. *The Open Classroom Reader*. New York: Random House.

SILVERSTEIN, S. 1974. *Where the Sidewalk Ends*. New York: Harper and Row.

SWANWICK, K. 1988. *Music, Mind, and Education*. London: Routledge.

VYGOTSKY, L. 1962, 1986. *Thought and Language*. Cambridge, Mass.: MIT Press.

WHITEHEAD, A. N. 1929. *The Aims of Education*. New York: Macmillan.